ESSENTIALS OF

EFFECTIVE

WRITING

A Practical Grammar and Handbook of Basic

Writing Techniques

VINCENT F. HOPPER / CEDRIC GALE

1906-

New York University

BARRON'S EDUCATIONAL SERIES, INC.

Great Neck, New York

203p.   20cm

(Barron's Educational series)

1. English language -- Grammar -- 1870 -
2. English language -- Rhetoric I. Gale,
Cedric, 1905 -   joint author II. Effective
writing III. t

Library of Congress Catalog Card Number: 61-8197

· CONTENTS

THE WORD

THE SENTENCE AND ITS PARTS

LOGIC AND CLARITY

EMPHASIS, CONSISTENCY, AND APPROPRIATENESS

PUNCTUATION

THE PARAGRAPH

THE WRITER'S APPROACH
TO HIS SUBJECT

· PREFACE

This book attempts to give the potential writer an expert command of the fundamentals of good English usage and the basic skills required for effective writing. In systematic fashion, it proceeds from analysis of English words to sentences. It continues with instruction on matters like logic, clarity, emphasis, consistency, and punctuation. It concludes with advice on handling the larger elements such as the paragraph and the whole composition.

ESSENTIALS OF EFFECTIVE WRITING may be studied as a course, proceeding from the simple to the more complex. The student may practice each principle in turn and be assured of his progress by using the companion volume PRACTICE FOR EFFECTIVE WRITING. If he has difficulty in spelling, Mersand's SPELLING YOUR WAY TO SUCCESS will complete the series he will require to become a dependable and effective writer.

The authors have also kept in mind the persistent need of writers for a compact ready reference work. Consequently, the diversified contents are clearly demarked and are readily identifiable to facilitate the finding of specific principles or answers to particular problems of composition. Instructors in the communication arts may refer students to specified numbered sections for guidance in their areas of weakness.

ESSENTIALS OF EFFECTIVE WRITING aims to be comprehensive without being cumbersome. It seeks, in all areas, to be exact, clear, succinct.

THE WORD

Just as an expert carpenter must be thoroughly acquainted with the tools of his craft and as an artist must have expert knowledge of colors, so a good writer must have a thorough understanding of the basic materials with which he works: words. Primitive peoples can get along with few and rather simple words. But the complex thoughts of civilized people require many words and words of several kinds, e.g., naming words, asserting words, connecting words, descriptive words. The first step to effective writing is therefore a knowledge of the properties and functions of the different kinds of words.

1 THE NOUN

The noun is the naming word. It is used to identify people, places, objects, ideas, emotions—in short, anything that can be named: *John, England, committee, table, truth, hatred, tennis.*

1A PROPER NOUNS

The individual title of any person, place, or thing is a proper noun. It is always capitalized. A good dictionary indicates proper nouns by capitalizing them. Some examples of proper nouns are: *James Madison High School, The Pine Tree Tavern, Crescent City, New York State, Negro, France, Mr. Smith, Judge Black.* Notice that words like *school* and *city* are capitalized when they are part of the title.

Titles of books, plays, themes, essays, etc. are similarly capitalized. The first word of the title is always capitalized and all other words except the articles (*a, an, the*) and short prepositions or conjunctions. The last word of the title is always capitalized: *Mourning Becomes Electra, The Mill on the Floss, A Rose for Emily, For Whom the Bell Tolls, Spring and Summer in Northern New England, He Got What He Asked For*.

The names of geographical regions are proper nouns: the *Southwest*, the *South*. These words are not proper nouns when they merely indicate direction.

He went *west*.

BUT   He settled in the *West*.

Other proper nouns include holidays (*Easter, Lincoln's Birthday*), days of the week (*Sunday, Monday*), months of the year (*January, February*)—but not the seasons (*winter, spring*).

Words which are ordinarily common nouns become proper nouns when they are used to identify a specific person, place, or thing. For example, *history* is a common noun, but *History of the United States* or *History 21* might be names of academic courses. *Mother* is a common noun in a phrase like *my mother*, but in the sentence *I will ask Mother*, the absence of the identifying word *my* makes *Mother* the identification or title of one specific person. In similar identifications like *Uncle John* or *President Smith*, the nouns *uncle* and *president* become proper nouns because they are a part of the identifications of specific people.

1 B COMMON NOUNS

Common nouns are the ordinary naming words to identify one or more of any type of person, place, or thing. With a few exceptions (like *wheat, statistics*), common nouns have number—singular and plural:

house   houses

mouse   mice

The singular of a common noun is unlimited and denotes all members of its class in the past, present, and future. The statement "*Man* was born to live in sorrow" refers to all members of the class of human beings.

The plural of a common noun is similarly unlimited: "*Plants* need sunshine."

The singular of a noun is limited to one member of its class by the use of the articles *a, an, the: a man, an apple, the plant.*

Subdivisions of a class are indicated by such words as *type, kind, sort, species, variety: a type of dress, a kind of flower.* Avoid such illogical usage as *a type of a dress.*

Plurals of nouns are similarly limited by the use of the definite article *the: the people, the elements.*

1C   POSSESSIVE CASE OF NOUNS

The possessive case of nouns, meaning *belonging to,* is usually formed by adding the apostrophe and *s* to words which do not end with an *s* or *z* sound and by adding only the apostrophe to words which end with an *s* or *z* sound:

> the boy's room   the children's school
>
> the boys' room   Dickens' novels

EXCEPTION: In words of one syllable ending in the *s* or *z* sound, it is customary to add the apostrophe and *s* and to pronounce the possessive as if it ended in *es: the boss's hat.*

To be certain about the correct placing of the apostrophe, remember that it always means *belonging to whatever immediately precedes it:*

> the boy's suit—belonging to the boy
> the boys' room—belonging to the boys
> the boss's office—belonging to the boss
> the bosses' office—belonging to the bosses
> the women's department—belonging to the women

1 D **When possession is shared by two or more nouns,** this fact is indicated by using the possessive case for the last noun in the series:

> John, Fred, and Edward's canoe

They all own the same canoe. If each one separately owns a canoe, each name is placed in the possessive case:

> John's, Fred's, and Edward's canoes

1 E **Inanimate objects are not capable of possession.** The relationship meaning *a part of* is indicated by the use of the preposition *of:*

> the wall of the castle NOT the castle's wall

EXCEPTIONS: Objects which are personified, such as ships and airplanes, do use the possessive case:

> the ship's compass   the plane's gyroscope

Idiomatic usage also allows the possessive case for time and money:

> a day's work   a dollar's worth   three years' time

In such instances, be careful in placing the apostrophe to observe whether the noun is singular or plural:

> a month's vacation   two months' vacation

2 THE PRONOUN

The pronoun is a word used in place of a noun. The noun for which the pronoun stands is called its antecedent. In the sentence *The dog lost its bone, its* is the pronoun; *dog* is the antecedent.

2 A   PERSONAL PRONOUNS

The personal pronouns are distinguished by person, case, and number.

FIRST PERSON (the person speaking or writing)

Case	Singular	Plural
Nominative	I	we
Possessive	my OR mine	our OR ours
Objective	me	us

SECOND PERSON (the person addressed)

Case	Singular	Plural
Nominative	you	you
Possessive	your OR yours	your OR yours
Objective	you	you

In the third person, pronouns are also distinguished by gender.
THIRD PERSON (the person, place, or thing spoken or written about)

Case	Singular			Plural
	Masculine	Feminine	Neuter	
Nominative	he	she	it	they
Possessive	his	her OR hers	its	their OR theirs
Objective	him	her	it	them

2 B   RELATIVE PRONOUNS

The relative pronouns, *who, which,* and *that,* are used to relate a dependent clause of a sentence to a word in the independent clause:

> The tools *which he used* were rusty.

The pronoun *who* is used to refer to persons; *which* refers to things, *that* refers to both persons and things. For references to persons it is preferable to use the pronoun *who* rather than *that*.

Like the personal pronouns, *who* takes different forms depending on its case.

Case	*Singular and Plural*
Nominative	who
Possessive	whose
Objective	whom

2 C INTERROGATIVE PRONOUNS

The interrogative pronouns, *who, which, what,* are used to ask a question. Their antecedents are the answers to the questions.

Who is the chairman?   ANSWER: John [the antecedent]

What is he carrying?   ANSWER: a suitcase [the antecedent]

Who as an interrogative pronoun is distinguished by case as above (2 B).

2 D DEMONSTRATIVE PRONOUNS

The demonstrative pronouns, *this* (singular), *these* (plural), *that* (singular), *those* (plural), are used to point out people, places, or things without naming them. The antecedent of a demonstrative pronoun is whoever or whatever is being pointed out.

I like *this*.   *Those* are good to eat.

2 E INDEFINITE PRONOUNS

The indefinite pronouns are so named because their antecedents are vague or unknown. These are such words as *each, all, either, anyone, somebody, everyone, whoever, whatever*. They form the possessive case in the same manner as nouns: *anyone's, somebody else's*.

2F INTENSIVE AND REFLEXIVE PRONOUNS

The intensive and reflexive pronouns, *myself* (singular), *ourselves* (plural), *yourself* (singular), *yourselves* (plural), *himself, herself, itself* (singular), *themselves* (plural), should never be used in a sentence without the corresponding personal pronouns or the nouns to which they refer. When used to intensify a noun or pronoun, they are known as intensive pronouns.

Mary *herself* was responsible. I *myself* will do it.

These pronouns are reflexive when they refer back to the subject.

I hurt *myself*. He did it to *himself*. They killed *themselves*.

2G USE OF THE NOMINATIVE CASE OF PRONOUNS

(1) The nominative case of *who* and of the personal pronouns is used when the pronoun is the subject of a verb.

I am tired.　　　*They* are coming.

Who is there?　　The man *who* was sick has recovered.

When these pronouns appear in comparisons using the conjunctions *as* and *than,* the verb is frequently understood.

He is older than *I* [am].

He plays as well as *I* [play].

When these pronouns answer a question, the verb is frequently understood.

Who is there? *I* [am].

(2) The nominative case is used when the pronoun follows any tense of the verb *to be* and is used as its complement.

It is *I* (*he, she, it, they*).

2 H USE OF THE OBJECTIVE CASE OF PRONOUNS

(1) The objective case is used when the pronoun is the object of a verb or a preposition.

John hit *her*. [object of verb *hit*]

Take the book from *him*. [object of preposition *from*]

Whom did you give it to? [object of preposition *to*]

(2) The objective case is used when the pronoun is the subject or object of an infinitive.

The judge expected *him* to be on time. (subject of infinitive *to be*)

Let the children have *them*. (object of infinitive *have*)

The minister asked *her* to see *me*. (subject and object)

2 I CASE OF PRONOUNS IN APPOSITION

Apposition means *placed beside*. To explain or define a word more fully, supplementary words may be placed in apposition to it, usually immediately following the word to be explained. In the phrase *we girls, girls* is in apposition to *we* to explain and define the pronoun. In the sentence *Three men approached the town, Jones, Smith, and I*, the words *Jones, Smith,* and *I* are in apposition to *men* even though they do not follow immediately.

When a pronoun is in apposition to a noun or another pronoun, it takes the same case as the word to which it is apposed.

The children, John, Eunice, and *I*, were all sick.

[*I* is in the same case as *children*—nominative because *children* is the subject of the sentence.]

Father sent for the children, John, Eunice, and *me*.

[*Me* is in the same case as *children*, objective because *children* is the object of the preposition *for*.]

Similarly, a word in apposition to a pronoun does not affect the case of the pronoun itself.

> *We* girls will be waiting for you.

> He waited for *us* girls.

A test for correctness is to rephrase the sentence using the pronoun alone.

> *We* [girls] will be waiting for you.

> He waited for *us* [girls].

> Father sent for [the children, John, Eunice, and] *me*.

3 THE VERB

The verb is a word which makes an assertion. Since an assertion must be made in connection with time (past, present, future), verbs are distinguished by tense. (See pp. 14-17.) A very few verbs like *ought* which do not possess a complete sequence of tenses are known as defective verbs. (For the conjugation of verbs, see pp. 188-191.) The basic forms of a verb are known as its principal parts:

> Infinitive: to see OR see
>
> Present Tense: see
>
> Present Participle: seeing
>
> Past Tense: saw
>
> Past Participle: seen

3A NUMBER AND PERSON

Verbs are distinguished by number (singular and plural) and by person (first, second, third). In general, verbs have a different form only in the third person singular of the present tense.

> I, you, we, they *move*.
>
> BUT   He, she, it *moves*.

An exception is the verb *to be* which is more highly inflected:

> SINGULAR: I *am;* you *are;* he, she, it *is*
>
> PLURAL: We, you, they *are*.

3 B MOOD

A verb may be placed in the indicative, imperative, or subjunctive mood to indicate differences in the intention of the speaker or writer.

The indicative mood is used to make an assertion or ask a question.

> The horse *galloped* down the street.
>
> Where *are* you *going?*

The imperative mood is used for commands, directions, or requests.

> COMMAND: *Go* to the store and *order* a typewriter.
>
> DIRECTION: *Turn* right at the next traffic light.
>
> REQUEST: Please *answer* my letter.

The form of the imperative mood is identical with that of the second person of the indicative mood except for the verb *to be* where it is *be*.

> *Be* good.   *Be* on time.   Please *be* cheerful.

3 C THE SUBJUNCTIVE MOOD

(1) The subjunctive mood of the verb is used to express a wish or a condition contrary to fact. This use of the subjunctive em-

ploys a special form only in the verb *to be;* the form is *were* for all persons.

WISH: I wish I *were* in Europe.

CONDITION CONTRARY TO FACT: If he *were* as good as he is clever, he would make an ideal leader.

(2) The subjunctive is also used in a dependent clause after a verb that expresses determination, a command, or a request. In this usage, the subjunctive form is the same as the infinitive, omitting the word *to.*

DETERMINATION: I insist that he *be* punctual.

COMMAND: I demand that he *see* me immediately.

REQUEST: I ask that my petition *be* granted.

(3) The same form of the subjunctive is occasionally used to indicate a dubious supposition.

If he *dare* do it, I shall be surprised.

If his report *be* confirmed, it will be a miracle.

(4) The same form of the subjunctive is used in parliamentary procedure to express a motion or a resolution.

Be it resolved that the secretary *keep* a record of the proceedings and *submit* it at the next meeting.

I move that the minutes *be* accepted as read.

3 D TRANSITIVE AND INTRANSITIVE VERBS

Verbs are classified as transitive or intransitive.

A transitive verb (*transit* means *to carry* as in *rapid transit*) requires an object to complete its meaning. The object of a transitive verb is affected, however slightly, by whatever the verb expresses:

The hammer *struck* the anvil.

[The object, *anvil,* has been hit.]

Angela *read* the newspaper.

[The object, *newspaper,* has been read.]

John *has* a horse.

[The object, *horse,* is owned.]

An intransitive verb makes an assertion without requiring any object.

The clock *strikes.*

He *walks* down the street every evening.

The bird *is* on the fence.

A copulative verb, a special kind of intransitive verb, is one which connects the subject to a noun, pronoun, or adjective in the predicate.

John *is* the president.

[*Is* connects *John* to *president. John* and *president* are the same person. A noun like *president* used after a copulative verb is called a predicate nominative. In the next two examples, *bluejay* and *I* are predicate nominatives.]

The bird *is* a bluejay.

It *is* I.

The most frequently used copulative verb is *to be.* Other commonly used copulative verbs are *become, seem, smell, look, grow, feel, sound, get, taste, appear.*

Many verbs are both transitive and intransitive. A good dictionary will indicate the differences in meaning. In *The hammer strikes the anvil,* the transitive verb *strike* means *to hit.* In a sentence such as *The clock strikes,* the intransitive verb *strike* means *to sound.* The transitive and intransitive meanings of the same verb may be similar, but they are never identical. The statement *He breathes* means that "he" is alive, but *He breathes the mountain air* refers to an experience which "he" is having.

3E VOICE

Transitive verbs are distinguished by voice, active and passive, to indicate whether the subject is the doer or the receiver of the action.

ACTIVE VOICE: John *ate* dinner.

John, the subject, is the actor or the doer. *Ate,* the verb, describes the action. *Dinner,* the object, is the receiver of the action.

PASSIVE VOICE: Dinner *was eaten* by John.

The passive voice, as in the above illustration, is formed by adding the appropriate form of the verb *to be* to the past participle of the transitive verb. When a verb is placed in the passive voice, the receiver of the action becomes the subject. The actor may be identified by the use of the preposition *by.*

The passive voice is used to emphasize or direct attention to the receiver of the action. In the sentence *A bus struck the young girl* (active voice), attention is directed to the bus. Putting the same statement in the passive voice, *The young girl was struck by the bus,* directs attention to the victim rather than to the type of vehicle which caused the accident.

The passive voice is also used to eliminate the necessity of naming the actor. (The instigator of the action might be unknown or unimportant or deliberately omitted for a variety of reasons.)

My uncle *was killed.*

His purse *was stolen.*

All the food *was eaten.*

3F THE PRESENT TENSE

(1) The present tense is used to state that something is so at the moment of speaking or writing.

> He *is* sick.   The apple *tastes* good.

(2) The present tense is used to assert a general truth or habitual action, regardless of time.

> Roses *smell* sweet.   Children *make* noise.

(3) The present tense may be used to refer to artistic productions of the past (in the sense that they are still extant) or to make assertions about artists (in the sense that they live as long as their works endure).

> Brahms *is* a well-known composer.
>
> Shakespeare *writes* in blank verse.

(4) The present tense is used (for the same reason) to narrate the plot of a fictional work.

> In Shakespeare's *Hamlet*, the opening scene *takes* place at night. Two sentries *are talking* . . .

The progressive form of the present tense is used to indicate continued or prolonged action or state of being. This effect is obtained by combining the verb *to be* with the present participle.

> I *am talking*. You *are listening*. We *are being* quiet.

The intensive form of the present tense is used to create an effect of decisiveness. The intensive form combines the verb *to do* with the infinitive.

> I *do study*.   He *does sing*.   They *do fly*.

3G THE FUTURE TENSE

The future tense is used to make an assertion about an anticipated event. Simple futurity is indicated by adding *shall* and *will*
to the infinitive. *Shall* is used for the first person and *will* for the
second and third persons.

> I (we) *shall go.*
>
> You *will go.*
>
> He (she, it, they) *will go.*

To indicate a promise or determination, *will* is used in the first
person: *I (we) will go.* To express a command or determination,
shall is used in the second and third persons: *You (he, she, it,
they) shall go.*

The progressive form also occurs in the future tense: *I (we)
shall be going. You (he, she, it, they) will be going.*

3H THE PAST TENSE

The past tense is used to assert that something occurred or ex-
isted at a definite time in the past.

> I *went* down the street yesterday.

The progressive and intensive forms occur in the past tense.

> PROGRESSIVE: I *was going.*
>
> INTENSIVE: I *did go.*

3I THE PRESENT PERFECT TENSE

The present perfect tense is formed by combining the verb *to
have* with the past participle.

> I *have gone.*   He *has gone.*

As its name indicates, the present perfect tense indicates a past event which is perfected or completed at the present time. Unlike the past tense, it does not refer to a definite time in the past. The statement *John went to Paris* (past tense) indicates a definite trip at a definite time in the past. But the statement *John has been in Paris* (present perfect tense) means only that taking one or several trips to Paris is *now* part of John's experience. Similarly, *I did it yesterday* (past tense) directs attention to a definite action at a definite time in the past. *I have done it* (present perfect tense) emphasizes only that the action is *now* completed. For this reason, the present perfect tense is also used to indicate an event or situation which began in the past and continued up to the present: *I have waited for you.*

The progressive form occurs in the present perfect tense.

He *has been going* to Paris for many years.

I *have been waiting* for you.

3 J   THE PAST PERFECT TENSE

The past perfect tense is formed by combining the past tense of the verb *to have* with the past participle. It indicates an event which was entirely perfected or completed at a definite time in the past.

By 1910 the Wright brothers *had invented* the airplane. [The invention occurred prior to 1910.]

The past perfect tense is generally used to indicate that in the past one event occurred before another.

Mary fell in the lake. She *had been* out in the canoe all morning.

The progressive form occurs in the past perfect tense.

They *had been looking* for him for a long time.

3 K THE FUTURE PERFECT TENSE

The future perfect tense is formed by combining the future tense of the verb *to have* with the past participle.

> I *shall have done* it. You *will have done* it.

It is used to indicate that an anticipated event will be perfected or completed before some definite time in the future.

> By sundown, he *will have finished* the job.

The progressive form occurs in the future perfect tense.

> He *will have been working* all afternoon.

4 THE ADJECTIVE AND THE ADVERB

Adjectives and adverbs are descriptive and limiting words.

4 A THE ADJECTIVE

The adjective is a word which modifies (describes or changes the meaning of) a noun or pronoun. The noun *man* refers to the entire human race, but the adjective *a* limits *man* to one male human being. The addition of other adjectives continues to limit as well as describe: *a tall, thin, intelligent man.* Adjectives derived from proper names are capitalized: *English, French.*

4 B THE ARTICLE

The most used adjectives are the articles, *a, an,* and *the. A* and *an* are called indefinite articles because they single out any one unspecified member of a class. *The* is called a definite article because it specifies a particular member or a particular group of members of a class.

A is used when it immediately precedes a word beginning with a consonant sound: *a book, a tree. An* is used when it immediately precedes a word beginning with a vowel sound: *an apple, an ancient city.*

NOTE: It is the sound, not the actual letter, which determines the form of the indefinite article: *a university, an R.C.A. television set, an 8-sided object.* In some instances when there are different pronunciations of the same word, the pronunciation used by the speaker or writer determines the form of the article. If the writer pronounces the word *humble* omitting the aspirant or h-sound, he should write *an humble person.* If he similarly omits the aspirant in *historical,* he should write *an historical novel.*

4 C THE PREDICATE ADJECTIVE

A predicate adjective is one which follows a copulative (linking) verb which joins it to the subject.

> The water is *hot.*
>
> The flowers smell *sweet.*
>
> The man is growing *old.*

As in these examples, the predicate adjective (*hot, sweet, old*) modifies the subject (*water, flowers, man*). Although adjectives usually precede the words they modify, the use of the predicate adjective makes it possible to convert a fact into a sentence or assertion.

> *hot water* (fact)—*The water is hot.* (assertion)

4 D THE ADVERB

The adverb is a word which modifies a verb, an adjective, or another adverb. For example, the adverb may modify a verb:

He entered the room *quietly*. [modifies the verb *entered*]

It may modify an adjective:

He was *truly* grateful. [modifies the adjective *grateful*]

It may modify another adverb:

She sang *extremely* well. [modifies the adverb *well*]

4 E   COMPARISON OF ADJECTIVES AND ADVERBS

Adjectives and adverbs have positive, comparative, and superlative forms. The positive form is the basic word (*kind, fast*). The comparative form indicates a comparison between two persons, places, things, or assertions.

He was *kinder* than his brother.

She ran *faster* than her mother.

The superlative form is used when more than two persons, places, things, or assertions are compared.

He was the *kindest* of all the children.

She ran the *fastest* of them all.

For adjectives of one syllable, the comparative is usually formed by adding *er* to the positive. The superlative is usually formed by adding *est*. For most adjectives of more than one syllable and for most adverbs, the comparative and superlative are formed by combining *more* and *most* with the positive.

POSITIVE	COMPARATIVE	SUPERLATIVE
small	smaller	smallest
beautiful	more beautiful	most beautiful
fast	faster	fastest
nobly	more nobly	most nobly

All adjectives and adverbs do not observe this principle. Observe:

POSITIVE	COMPARATIVE	SUPERLATIVE
little	littler	littlest
bad	worse	worst
ill	worse	worst
well	better	best

When in doubt, consult a good dictionary.

4 F   CONFUSION OF ADJECTIVES AND ADVERBS

Some words like *fast, slow, very, late* function as either adjectives or adverbs depending on what they modify.

ADJECTIVE: It was a *fast* train. [modifies noun *train*]

ADJECTIVE: The clock was *fast*. [modifies noun *clock*]

ADVERB: The horse ran *fast*. [modifies verb *ran*]

The following adjectives and adverbs are sometimes confused: *good, well, bad, badly. Good* is an adjective and must modify a noun or pronoun.

He was a *good* man. [modifies noun *man*]

I feel *good*. [modifies pronoun *I*]

Well is an adjective meaning in good health and may be substituted for *good* in the preceding examples. But *well* is also an adverb meaning in a satisfactory or superior manner.

He played *well*. [modifies verb *played*]

He was *well* aware of his plight. [modifies adjective *aware*]

The adverb *badly* is sometimes mistaken for the adjective *bad*, meaning in poor spirits, in such sentences as *John feels bad, You look bad*. In both of these sentences, the adjective *bad* describes the condition of the subject (*John, you*). Never write: *I feel badly*.

When an adjective follows a copulative verb (like *is, feel, look, seem, become, smell*), it modifies the subject and is known as a predicate adjective.

The water is (seems, feels, looks, is getting, is becoming) *hot.*

I feel (look, am) *fine, ill, sick, good, bad.*

5 THE VERBAL

In addition to the forms of the verb described in Section 3, there is a group of words known as verbals. These words are derived from verbs but, unlike the finite verbs, they do not indicate definite time nor are they limited in person and number. Although they act partly as verbs (they may have complements and adverbial modifiers), they also function simultaneously as other parts of speech. The verbals consist of the present and present perfect infinitives, the present and present perfect participles, and the past and past perfect participles.

5A THE INFINITIVE

The forms of the infinitives are the present infinitive (*to be, to do*) and the perfect infinitive (*to have been, to have done*). The progressive form also occurs: *to be doing, to have been doing.* The *to* is sometimes omitted as a matter of idiomatic usage: *Let me do it. (Ask me to do it.)*

Infinitives usually function as nouns. (See Sec. 9C) In the sentence *Life is good,* the noun *life* can be replaced by the infinitive *to live.* While functioning as nouns they may also, like verbs, have modifiers and complements:

To live happily is desirable.

[subject of verb *is* and modified by adverb *happily*]

To play Bach was her lifetime ambition.

[*Bach* is the object of the infinitive *to play; to play Bach* is the subject of *was.*]

5B THE GERUND

The gerund is a present participle that functions as a noun and therefore names an action or a state of being. Like the infinitive, it may have modifiers and complements.

> *Swimming* is good exercise.
>
> *Eating* too much is bad for one's health.
>
> *Being* gloomy was habitual to her.
>
> *Bowling* on the green was his favorite sport.

5C THE PRESENT AND PRESENT PERFECT PARTICIPLES

The present and present perfect participles (with or without complements and modifiers) function as adjectives.

> The *dying* man. The *falling* star. [modify *man* and *star*]
>
> *Having slept,* he felt rested. [modifies *he*]

The present perfect participle is formed by combining *having* with the past participle. It refers to an event already completed at the time expressed by its related verb.

> *Having learned* his lesson, he was a better man.

5D THE PAST AND PAST PERFECT PARTICIPLES

The past and past perfect participles (with or without complements and modifiers) function as adjectives. They are used to describe an action happening *to* the noun or pronoun being modified.

The child, *bitten* by the dog, cried bitterly.

[The past participle *bitten* modifies *child* and describes something that happened to him.]

Seen under neon lights, the dress looked purple.

[The past participle *seen* modifies *dress* and describes the fact that it was looked at.]

The past perfect participle is formed by combining *having been* with the past participle. It indicates an action already completed at the time expressed by its related verb.

Having been discovered, the thief confessed.

 THE PREPOSITION

The preposition is a connecting word that is used to relate one word to another. The word *preposition* means *placed before;* it is so named because it always precedes a noun or a pronoun (or their equivalent—any group of words acting as a noun).

The book is *on* the desk.

My hat is *like* yours.

Common prepositions are: *about, after, among, around, at, before, below, beside, between, by, down, for, from, in, inside, into, like, of, on, over, to, toward, under, up, upon, within.*

 THE CONJUNCTION

The conjunction (meaning *joined with*) is a connecting word which joins words, phrases, or clauses.

7 A COORDINATING CONJUNCTIONS

Coordinating conjunctions join sentence elements of equal importance. The coordinating conjunctions are *and, but, or, nor, for, whereas, yet.* They may join a word to another word (*bread and butter*), a phrase to another phrase (*into the oven or over the fire*), an independent clause to another independent clause (*He wanted to learn, but he hated to study*), a dependent clause to another dependent clause (*Matilda came in after I arrived but before dinner was served*).

The coordinating conjunctions are occasionally used effectively to introduce a sentence.

He said he would do it. *And* he did.

She swore that she told the truth. *Yet* she lied.

7 B CORRELATIVE CONJUNCTIONS

Correlative conjunctions are pairs of words used to join sentence elements of equal importance. They are words like *both . . . and, either . . . or, neither . . . nor, not only . . . but also.*

7 C SUBORDINATING CONJUNCTIONS

Subordinating conjunctions join sentence elements of unequal rank. Common subordinating conjunctions are: *as, after, although, because, before, if, since, that, though, unless, until, when, where, while.*

Subordinating conjunctions are most frequently used to join dependent clauses to independent clauses.

He whistled *while* he worked.

The relative pronouns (*who, which, that*) frequently act as subordinating conjunctions:

John, *who* was ill, recovered.

When indicating a causal relationship, the conjunctions *because*, *since*, and *as* are preferable in that order. *Since* is weaker than *because*, for it also refers to time (*She has been unhappy since her last child was born*). *As* is the weakest because it also refers both to time and comparison (*He tackled each problem as he came to it. He played as hard as he worked*).

7D CONFUSION OF PREPOSITIONS AND CONJUNCTIONS

A few words like *after* function both as prepositions and conjunctions

> He came *after* me. [preposition]

> He left *after* I did. [conjunction]

The conjunctions *as* and *than* are sometimes confused with prepositions because they frequently introduce elliptical clauses (clauses where words are omitted because the meaning is clear without them).

> He worked as rapidly *as* I [worked].

> I worked more rapidly *than* he [worked].

> She disliked him as much *as* [she disliked] me.

> The rain soaked him more *than* [it soaked] me.

The verbs are not stated in these examples, but the fact that they are understood requires the use of conjunctions rather than prepositions.

Do not confuse the preposition *like* with the conjunction *as*. Since it is a preposition, *like* should never precede a clause (subject and verb).

> *As* I was saying   NOT   *Like* I was saying

> *As* you were   NOT   *Like* you were

THE INTERJECTION

Interjections (the word means *thrown in*) are words which do not fulfill any of the functions of the previous parts of speech. They are such words as *yes, no, oh, ah, well, hello*. Although they are frequently used in sentences, they are not properly parts of sentence structure and are therefore separated from the remainder of the sentence by punction marks.

> *Oh,* I didn't see you.
>
> *Yes.* I shall do it.
>
> I waited, *alas,* too long.
>
> *No!* You can't mean it.

·THE SENTENCE
AND ITS PARTS

The sentence is the unit of expression that conveys a thought. A mere group of words like

The boy throwing the ball

puzzles the reader and makes him ask, "What about the boy throwing the ball? But a sentence like

The boy threw the ball.

satisfies the reader by telling him what the boy did. The sentence is explicit. Whether short or long, simple or intricate, the sentence conveys a complete thought.

THE SENTENCE DEFINED

A sentence is a group of words that contains a subject and a predicate, expresses a complete thought and ends with a period (.), a question mark (?), or an exclamation point (!).

She is pretty.

In this province the rivers and creeks were the only routes from settlement to settlement.

Who now can foretell the effects of atomic fallout on future generations?

How wonderful it is to see again!

9 A THE SUBJECT

The subject of a sentence is the part about which something is said.

> *The delegate* arrived this morning.
>
> *The child* is crying for his mother.

The simple subject is the principal noun or its equivalent. The *complete subject* is the simple subject plus all of the words related to it.

In the following sentences the simple subject is capitalized and the complete subject is italicized.

> *My FATHER* works for E. L. Lanyard and Company.
>
> *Another SOURCE of annoyance and disappointment* is the weakness of the public members of the board.

The subject of an interrogative sentence is the part about which the question is asked. The subject of an interrogative sentence can often be identified by recasting the sentence as a statement.

> Has *MOTHER* telephoned today? [MOTHER has telephoned today.]
>
> Is salary *the PROBLEM now being considered by the sub-committee?* [*The PROBLEM now being considered by the sub-committee* is salary.]

In commands and directions the subject is frequently omitted because it is readily understood.

> [YOU] Lay up your treasure in heaven.
>
> [YOU] Shift into low gear on a long downgrade.

A compound subject is one that contains two or more simple subjects joined by the conjunctions *and, or,* or by other coordinating or correlative conjunctions.

The DRIVERS and LOADERS have threatened to strike.

Either the FROST or the shortened DAY makes the leaves turn red in the autumn.

Not only the PRICE but also the QUALITY of their products fluctuates wildly.

The subject is normally placed at the beginning of the sentence, but it may be placed after the predicate or between parts of the predicate.

The COMPANY of just and righteous men is better than wealth and a rich estate.

Precious in the sight of the Lord is *the DEATH of His saints.*

If you wish me to weep, *YOU yourself* must feel grief.

9 B THE PREDICATE

The predicate of a sentence is the part that makes the statement or asks the question.

Haydn *wrote over a hundred symphonies.*

Will the development of guided missles *radically change the mode of warfare?*

The simple predicate is the principal verb of the sentence. It may be a single verb or a verb phrase.

> The dog *barked.*

> The dog *has been barking.*

A compound predicate is one that contains two or more simple predicates joined by *and, or,* or by other coordinating or correlative conjunctions.

> She *PLAYS the piano and SINGS.*

> He *REPAID the money or PROMISED to repay it.*

The predicate is normally placed after the subject, but it may precede the subject or enclose it. The predicate can be identified, not by its position, but by its function in the sentence: that of saying something about the subject. Regardless of its position in the sentence, a group of words belongs to the predicate if it helps to make an assertion about the subject.

The following sentences illustrate some of the patterns the predicate may follow:

The new German tenor *will sing the role of Tristan.*

If he lives up to advance notices, he *will be the best Tristan heard here in more than a decade.*

There on the topmost limb of the tree sat Tommy.

Had she *already spoken when we first saw her with Martin?*

Here end my quotations from this very unusual and perhaps somewhat insolent letter.

9 C PHRASES

Phrases are closely knit groups of words that lack a subject and a predicate and function as a unit. They may therefore be contained in a sentence but do not in themselves make a complete statement.

The following groups of words are phrases:

in the morning

calling the manager

to sell the estate

There are five principal kinds of phrases:

(1) A *prepositional phrase* is introduced by a preposition and is used as an adjective or an adverb to modify some other word in the sentence.

Men *of good will* are benefactors of humanity. [*Of good will* is an adjective phrase modifying *men*.]

Stop *at the count of ten*. [*At the count of ten* is an adverbial phrase modifying the verb *stop*.]

(2) *A participial phrase* is introduced by a participal and is used as an adjective to modify a noun or a pronoun.

Holding the dog by its collar, the boy refused to go.

[*Holding the dog by its collar* is a present participial phrase modifying *boy*.]

Pulled tight across the frame, the material looked more lustrous. [*Pulled tight across the frame* is a past participial phrase modifying *material*.]

(3) An *infinitive phrase* is introduced by the infinitive form of the verb, usually preceded by *to*. An infinitive phrase is used as a noun, adjective, or adverb, and partially as a verb.

To serve humanity was our desire. [*To serve humanity* is a noun phrase used as the subject of *was*.]

They were determined *to break* the rules. [*To break* is partially a verb and takes an object, *rules*.]

He has a bone *to pick*. [*To pick* is used as an adjective to modify the noun *bone*.]

The dish was too hot *to handle*. [*To handle* is used as an adverb to modify the adjective *hot*.]

(4) A *verb phrase* is a group of related verbs that functions as a unit.

You *may go;* I *can go* next time.

By next October I *shall have been living* here twenty years.

[*Shall have been living* is the future perfect tense of the verb *to live*.]

(5) A *gerund phrase* is introduced by a gerund and is used as a noun, i.e., as subject, object, complement, or appositive.

Using profane language is not permitted in this place. [*Using profane language* is a gerund phrase used as the subject of the verb *is.*]

9 D CLAUSES

A clause is a group of words that contains a subject and a predicate and is used as part of a sentence. A clause is always a sub-division of a sentence.

In the following sentences the clauses are set off by parentheses:

(*He is the man*) (*who spoke to me.*)

(*I called after him,*) (*but he did not hear.*)

INDEPENDENT CLAUSES

An independent clause (also called a major or main clause) makes a grammatically complete statement and could therefore be written as a sentence.

In the following sentences the independent clauses are italicized and are then rewritten in brackets to show that they can stand alone as complete and independent units of thought.

After the hard day's work, *I was exhausted.* [I was exhausted.]

The director scolded, and the actors sulked. [The director scolded. And the actors sulked.]

Mrs. Butler spends lavishly; she has an independent income. [Mrs. Butler spends lavishly. She has an independent income.]

DEPENDENT CLAUSES

A dependent clause (also called a subordinate or minor clause) does not express a complete thought and therefore cannot stand alone. Instead of expressing a complete thought, a dependent clause usually qualifies the thought of an independent clause. Hence a dependent clause usually relies on an independent clause for full significance and is related to some word in the independent clause.

The following clauses are dependent and incomplete:

unless the armaments race is abandoned

because there are defects in the basic structure

that we submitted last week

These dependent clauses can be given significance by being properly related to independent clauses. In the following illustrations the independent clauses are italicized.

Unless the armaments race is abandoned, *the nations will be bankrupt.*

The Severing Bridge is weak because there are defects in its basic structure.

The bid that we submitted last week *has been returned unopened.*

Dependent clauses are used as nouns, adjectives, and adverbs.

NOUN CLAUSES	They hoped *that the war would end soon.* [Object of the verb *hoped.*]
	How he escaped was not stated in the report. [Subject of the sentence.]
ADJECTIVE CLAUSES	We require men *who have proved their ability.* [Modifies the noun *men.*]
	Parents *who are over-indulgent* spoil their children. [Modifies the noun *parents.*]

ADVERBIAL
CLAUSES

I am so happy *that I could sing.* [Modifies the adjective *happy.*]

We should answer *when mother calls.* [Modifies the verb *should answer.*]

Below is a list of the principal subordinating words used to introduce dependent clauses. Clauses introduced by these words are always dependent.

(1) Relative and interrogative pronouns

who	which
what	that

(2) Subordinate conjunctions

TIME

until	while
when	as
since	before

PLACE

where	whence

CONDITION

if	provided that
unless	in case that

CONCESSION

though	even if
if	although

CAUSE

as	because
since	inasmuch as

MANNER

as	as if
like	though

9E TYPES OF SENTENCES

According to the number and kinds of clauses that sentences contain, they are classified as *simple, complex, compound,* and *compound-complex* sentences.

A *simple sentence* is one that contains no clauses.

> Facts are stubborn things.

> No path of flowers leads to glory.

A *complex sentence* contains *one independent clause* and *one or more dependent clauses.* In the following sentences the dependent clauses are italicized.

> The veracity *which increases with old age* is not far from folly.

> There are few people *who would not be ashamed of being loved when they love no longer.*

A *compound sentence* contains *two or more independent clauses,* but *no dependent clauses.*

> *Good wits jump; a word to the wise is enough.*

> *There the wicked cease from troubling; and the weary be at rest.*

A *compound-complex sentence* is a combination of the compound sentence and the complex sentence; that is, it contains *two or more independent clauses* and *one or more dependent clauses.* In the following examples the dependent clauses are italicized:

> Individualities may form communities, but it is institutions alone *that can create a nation.*

> Sometimes the little ship looked like a moving van *as she rolled on down the river,* and I could hardly see to steer because of the miscellaneous mountain of stuff on her flat-top deck.

10 SENTENCE FRAGMENTS

A sentence fragment is a phrase or a dependent clause written as if it were a sentence.

As we have seen, phrases and dependent clauses are incomplete; they cannot stand alone as sentences because they do not express complete thoughts. Both phrases and clauses are merely qualifying elements that must be properly related to sentences in order to gain significance. To write a phrase or a dependent clause as if it were a sentence is therefore to violate the logic of thought. Every sentence fragment is a failure in thought; it is a confession that the writer is not thinking or does not know how to think.

Written below are a number of different kinds of sentence fragments. Note that none has a subject or a predicate or expresses a thought. Each fragment leaves the reader in suspense, asking, "Well, what about it?" With this test of common sense, anyone should be able to detect any sentence fragment, even if he knows nothing at all about the requirements of a sentence. Try your ear and mind on the following:

Early in the morning before the sun had risen above the horizon.

While he was serving his residency at the hospital.

Leaping and bounding through the air with amazing dexterity.

To serve my God and my country to the best of my ability.

Who served with distinction in the armed forces.

10 A Do not write a dependent clause as if it were a complete sentence.

There are two ways of correcting this kind of sentence fragment: (1) by removing the subordinating word or (2) by properly relating the dependent clause to an independent clause.

DEPENDENT CLAUSE	That we should be allowed to travel freely abroad.
SENTENCE (1)	We should be allowed to travel freely abroad.
SENTENCE (2)	Has the Supreme Court ruled that we should be allowed to travel freely abroad?
DEPENDENT CLAUSE	While millions of people all over the world are dying of starvation.
SENTENCE (1)	Millions of people all over the world are dying of starvation.
SENTENCE (2)	We have an abundance of food while millions of people all over the world are dying of starvation.

10 B Do not write a gerund phrase or a participial phrase as it it were a sentence.

There are two ways of correcting this kind of fragment: (1) by changing the gerund or participial phrase into a finite verb and adding a subject, or (2) by properly relating the phrase to a sentence.

PHRASE	Giving an aggressive nation whatever it demands.
SENTENCE (1)	*Give* an aggressive nation whatever it demands.
SENTENCE (2)	*I do not advocate* giving an aggressive nation whatever it demands.
PHRASE	Believing in equal opportunity for all.
SENTENCE (1)	*I believe* in equal opportunity for all.
SENTENCE (2)	Believing in equal opportunity for all, *I am an advocate of a strong civil rights bill.*

PHRASE	Waiting in the freezing cold for over an hour.
SENTENCE (1)	*I waited* in the freezing cold for over an hour.
SENTENCE (2)	Waiting in the freezing cold for over an hour, *John suffered a severe chill.*

10 C **Do not write an infinitive phrase as if it were a complete thought.**

There are two ways of correcting this kind of fragment: (1) by turning the infinitive into a finite verb and adding a subject, if necessary, and (2) by properly relating the infinitive phrase to the sentence.

PHRASE	To hear Beethoven's piano sonatas played by a great pianist.
SENTENCE (1)	*I have heard* Beethoven's piano sonatas played by a great pianist.
SENTENCE (2)	To hear Beethoven's piano sonatas played by a great pianist *is a rare experience.*

PHRASE	To read a foreign language fluently.
SENTENCE (1)	*Can you read* a foreign language fluently?
SENTENCE (2)	*It is not easy* to read a foreign language fluently.

10 D **Do not write a prepositional phrase as if it were a complete sentence.**

This kind of sentence fragment can be corrected by properly relating the phrase to a sentence.

PHRASE   In New England, the deep South, and even in the Northwest.

SENTENCE   *I have lived in widely separate sections of the United States*—in New England, the deep South, and even in the Northwest.

PHRASE   First as a stock boy, and then as a mailclerk, a teller, and an auditor.

SENTENCE   *I have worked for the Dockside National Bank in several capacities,* first as a stock boy, and then as a mailclerk, a teller, and an auditor.

10 E   Do not write an appositive as if it were a complete sentence.

The appositive should be placed in the sentence to which it belongs.

APPOSITIVE   A brilliant, hard-driving man who will not tolerate slackness.

SENTENCE   *The greatest influence on my life has been my Uncle Oscar,* a brilliant, hard-driving man who will not tolerate slackness.

10 F   Do not write one member of a compound predicate as if it were a complete sentence.

Place the member of the compound predicate in the sentence to which it belongs.

FRAGMENT   And has been knocked out in the third round by the superannuated Tornado Barnes.

SENTENCE   *Since coming to this country Pepe Flores has lost two decisions* and has been knocked out in the third round by the superannuated Tornado Barnes.

10 G THE PROPER USE OF SENTENCE FRAGMENTS

There are several proper uses for sentence fragments:

(1) In informal speaking and hence in written dialogue

"Catch anything?"

"A couple of pickerel."

"Good size?"

"Fair. About twenty, twenty-one inches long."

(2) For exclamations

Finished!

Goodness gracious!

(3) For rhetorical effect

What marks the arrival of spring in the city? *A line of old ladies abloom in the park. Resurrection and life eternal! Old ladies reborn from cold-winter flats, sitting in rows and clusters and gayly nodding at passers-by.*

Professional writers often use intentional fragments effectively, *but the beginner should never use them.* The beginner should first master the sentence and know what effects he can and cannot achieve with it before he assumes the liberties taken by experienced craftsmen. Moreover, fragments are most advantageously used in fiction and in various forms of loose and unconventional prose that one should attempt only after he has learned the fundamentals of English composition and the principles of expository writing.

11 THE COMMA FAULT

The comma fault or comma splice is the error of placing a comma at the end of a sentence and beginning the next sentence without a capital letter.

11 A End each sentence with a period, a question mark, or an exclamation point, and begin the next sentence with a capital letter.

COMMA FAULT   The train is very late, we have been waiting for over an hour.

CORRECT   The train is very late. We have been waiting for over an hour.

COMMA FAULT   The President immediately vetoed the bill, the Congress promptly passed it over his veto!

CORRECT   The President immediately vetoed the bill. The Congress promptly passed it over his veto!

CORRECT   The President immediately vetoed the bill; the Congress promptly passed it over his veto!

11 B Use a comma between two independent clauses joined by the coordinating conjunctions *and*, *but*, *for*, *or*, *nor*, *whereas*, *yet*, *either . . . or*, and *neither . . . nor*.

Eugene O'Neill wrote *Desire Under the Elms*, and the Theatre Guild produced it.

Man proposes, *but* God disposes.

Do not ship the material, *for* I shall be abroad all summer.

However, if the independent clauses themselves contain commas, use a semicolon to indicate the end of one independent clause and the beginning of the next.

Eugene O'Neill, who is, I believe, regarded as our greatest playwright, wrote *Desire Under the Elms;* and the Theatre Guild produced it.

He tried every size, every color, and every variety; but none, not even the sample you submitted, was satisfactory.

11 C Use a semicolon between two independent clauses that are not joined by a connecting word or phrase.

By boat the journey takes three days; by jet airplane it takes eight hours.

He is an electronic engineer; he designs and builds mechanical computers.

11 D Use a semicolon between independent clauses joined by the conjunctive adverbs *however, then, nevertheless, therefore, consequently,* etc.

Lever House has been praised by most architects; however, it does not appeal to me.

He has not paid his dues for over a year; consequently, we must cancel his membership.

The Dodgers and the Braves have had a poor season; nevertheless, their fans remain loyal.

11 E Use the following diagrams to help you avoid the comma fault by punctuating sentences and independent clauses correctly.

_____.	_____.
sentence	sentence

_____;	_____.
independent clause	independent clause

_____,	and but for or nor whereas yet	_____.
independent clause		independent clause

___,___,___;	and but for or nor whereas yet	___,___,___,___.
independent clause with modifiers		independent clause with modifiers

···,	_____.
dependent clause	independent clause

_____	···.
independent clause	dependent clause

11 F Use the rules set forth in this section even though you have seen some comma splices in the work of eminent writers.

Through years of practice, the skilled writer knows when he can break rules to good effect. Until you have gained this knowledge, however, you use the comma fault at the risk of obscurity and illiteracy.

12   THE FUSED SENTENCE

A fused sentence consists of two sentences that are indistinguishably run together; the first sentence does not end with a mark of punctuation, and the second sentence does not begin with a capital letter.

The fused sentence is the most serious violation of logic and clarity that a writer can commit. It shows that he is incapable of sorting out his thoughts and recognizing where one thought ends and the next one begins. As a result, the reader is often confused and misled. He is forced to reread the sentence and even then he may not always be sure of the writer's intention.

12 A   Avoid fused sentences by ending every sentence with the proper mark of terminal punctuation and beginning the next sentence with a capital letter.

FUSED   With a mighty blow I struck my opponent fell to the ground.

CORRECT   With a mighty blow I struck. My opponent fell to the ground.

FUSED   There is no denying that on his trip abroad the Ambassador talked foolishly to the populace he was an international joke.

CORRECT   There is no denying that on his trip abroad the Ambassador talked foolishly to the populace. He was an international joke.

12 B   Avoid fused sentences by connecting and punctuating independent clauses according to the rules set forth in Section 11E on the comma fault.

· LOGIC AND CLARITY

13 AGREEMENT OF SUBJECT AND VERB

When words with number, person, and gender are related, they must agree in form. A verb must agree with its subject in number and person. The principle of agreement can be illustrated by the conjugation of any verb in the present tense.

Person	Singular	Plural
First	I talk	We talk
Second	You talk	You talk
Third	He, She, It talks	They talk

Since person causes little difficulty, the rule of agreement of subject and verb can be simply expressed: *a singular subject requires a singular verb, and a plural subject requires a plural verb.* To apply this rule, however, one must be able to identify a subject (see Sec. 9A) and to determine its number.

13 A Use a singular verb when the subject is a singular pronoun.

Special care must be taken to use a singular verb with *each, every, anybody, anyone, nobody, no one, someone, either,* and *neither,* even if they are followed by a plural noun.

Each of the sofas *is* over ninety inches long.

As yet *nobody has challenged* my theory.

Everybody has his price, the cynic believes.

Somebody across the street *plays* the trombone.

NOTE: Use a singular verb with *some, most,* and *none* when they mean quantity or bulk; use a plural verb when they mean units or numbers.

Some of the cereal *is* wormy. [*Cereal* is one bulk.]

Some of the apples *are* rotten. [*Apples* are individual units.]

None of the plaster *has* hardened, and *none* of the walls *have been painted.* [*Plaster* is bulk or quantity, but *walls* are units.]

Some authorities insist that *none* is more commonly used with the plural verb and therefore prefer the use of *no one* when the meaning is singular.

None of the buildings are original in design.

No one of the buildings is original in design.

13 B   Use a plural verb with *many, several, few, a variety,* and *a number* when they mean objects and people.

Several have been tested.

Many are called, but *few are* chosen.

A *variety* of fish *abound* in these waters.

13 C   Make the verb agree with the subject, not with a modifier of the subject.

A *herd* of sheep *is* crossing the road. [*Of sheep* is the plural modifier of the singular subject *herd.*]

The *men* in the district office *have organized* a ball team.

[*In the district office* is the singular modifier of the plural subject *men.*]

13 D   Use a plural verb when a subject is composed of two or more coordinate nouns (a compound subject).

Mink and *sable are* expensive furs.

The *senator* and his *wife were* warmly received.

NOTE: A singular verb is used when the coordinate nouns refer to the same person or thing.

A *scholar* and a *gentleman is* what he strives to be. [One person.]

This *prelude* and *fugue is* by Bach. [One composition.]

A singular verb is also used when *every* or *each* precede two coordinate nouns.

Every boy and *every girl has* received a present.

13 E   Use a singular verb with singular nouns joined by *either . . . or* or *neither . . . nor.*

Either the muffler or the *engine pipe was* replaced.

Neither time nor prosperity has softened his heart.

When *either . . . or* or *neither . . . nor* joins singular and plural nouns, the verb agrees with the nearer noun.

Either the *cloth* or the *dyes are* defective. [*Dyes* is nearer.]

Neither the *president nor* his *advisors have acted* wisely in the present crisis. [*Advisors* is nearer.]

13 F   Make the verb agree with the subject, not with a parenthetical expression introduced by *with, together with, as well as,* and the like.

Cezanne's "*Judgment of Paris*," together with several Miro's, *is hung* in the south gallery.

The *mayor*, as well as the councilmen, *has been implicated.*

Parenthetical expressions of this kind are phrases that do not affect the number of the subject. Parenthetical expressions may also be introduced by *along with, including, in addition to,* and *no less than.*

13 G Make the verb agree with the subject, not with the predicate nominative.

The greatest nuisance *is* the *refunds* we have to make. [*Nuisance* governs the verb. *Refunds* is a predicate nominative.]

The children of today *are* the hope of tomorrow. [*Children* governs the verb. *Hope* is a predicate nominative.]

NOTE that if these sentences are reversed, the number of the verb must be changed.

The refunds we have to make *are* the greatest nuisance. [*Refunds* now governs the verb, and *nuisance* is the predicate nominative.]

The hope of tomorrow *is* the children of today. [*Hope* now governs the verb, and *children* is the predicate nominative.]

13 H Use a singular or a plural verb with a collective noun according to the meaning intended.

If a group is regarded as a unit, the collective noun is singular and requires a singular verb.

The *orchestra performs* well under any conductor. [The orchestra plays as a unit.]

The *army marches* up the hill and then *marches* down again. [The army moves as a unit.]

If the members of a group are considered individually, the collective noun is plural and requires a plural verb.

After the trial the *jury were* threatened with violence. [Individual jurors received threats.]

The *family were* informed as soon as they could be reached by telephone. [Individual members of the family were apprised.]

13 1 **Use a singular verb with most nouns that are plural in form, but singular in meaning.**

Usually singular: *measles, mumps, billiards, news, economics, mathematics, logistics, linguistics.*

> *Measles is* a disease of childhood.

> The *news is* good tonight.

Usually plural: *trousers, tongs, wages, tactics, pliers, scissors, odds, glasses, barracks, insignia.*

> My *trousers are* badly frayed at the cuffs.

> The *wages* of sin *are* death.

Singular or plural, depending on meaning: *accoustics, gymnastics, ethics, politics, statistics, acrobatics.* These nouns are singular in meaning when they denote organized fields of knowledge or activity.

> *Politics has* always attracted men of great talent.

> *Statistics is* a dull, dry subject.

These nouns are plural in all other uses.

> The *statistics are* largely erroneous.

> His *ethics have* been questioned.

NOTE: Quoted literary titles and the plural names of organizations are always singular.

Two Gentlemen of Verona is a play by Shakespeare.

Hitz, Hall, and Murphy has announced a reorganization.

13 J Use a singular verb with plural subjects that represent mass, quantity, fractions, multiples, etc. when the subject is regarded as a unit.

Two-thirds of the sweater *has* been completed. [One sweater]

Ten per cent of the men drafted *are* over thirty. [Several individuals]

Fifty dollars is too much for that suit. [One amount]

Sometimes either a singular or a plural verb is permissible. However, it is less confusing to use the singular form consistently.

Two plus two is (*are*) *four*. [The sum *is*.]

Two times two is (*are*) *four*. [The product *is*.]

13 K Use *there is* before a singular noun or pronoun: use *there are* before a plural noun or pronoun.

There is no *clue* to the meaning of this cypher.

There are several *witnesses* to be heard.

The subjects of these sentences are *clue* and *witnesses* respectively. *There* is neither logically nor grammatically related to the sentence. *There* is used to change the word order of the sentence; it is a filler that is used for smoothness and emphasis. This kind of word is called an *expletive*. In the sentence *It is rumored that he is about to resign, it* is also an expletive.

13 L Use a plural verb with a relative pronoun which refers to a plural antecedent.

She is one of those militant *feminists who have* sacrificed *their* lives for woman's rights. [*Who* is a plural pronoun and requires a plural verb because it refers to the plural antecedent *feminists*.]

He made one of those tactless *remarks which make* everyone blush with embarrassment. [*Which* is plural and requires a plural verb because it refers to the plural antecedent *remarks.*]

13 M Use *does not* or *doesn't* (not *don't*) with a subject in the third person singular.

The President *does not* like to hold press conferences. [Never write *the President don't.*]

14 AGREEMENT OF PRONOUN AND ANTECEDENT

A pronoun must be in the same person, number, and gender as its antecedent, the noun or pronoun to which it refers.

Mr. Riggs said that *he* would accept the chairmanship if someone were appointed to assist *him.*

In this sentence the pronouns *he* and *him* are in the third person, masculine gender, and singular number to agree with their antecedent, *Mr. Riggs.* Note, however, that *him* is in the objective case and does not agree with *Mr. Riggs,* which is in the nominative case. The case of a pronoun is determined by its function in the sentence and not by its antecedent. (See Sec. 16)

These principles of agreement must always be clearly and consistently applied. The antecedent noun or pronoun must be clearly stated, and the pronouns referring to it must be in the same number, person, and gender.

14 A Use a singular pronoun to refer to indefinite singular antecedents.

These antecedents are the indefinite pronouns *each, every, everyone, everybody, any, anyone, anybody, either, neither,* etc. (See Sec. 2E)

Give to *each* according to *his* need.

Everyone raised *his* voice in song.

NOTE: The masculine pronoun is generally used when both sexes are involved. It is unnecessary and awkward to write:

Nobody can buy *his* or *her* way to happiness.

Except in the most formal writing, *he, him, his* are used to refer to the indefinite pronoun *one* and to other indefinite antecedents.

One must not waste *his* time in idleness. [Preferred]

One must not waste *one's* time in idleness. [Formal, stilted.]

14 B Use a plural pronoun with two or more singular antecedents joined by *and*.

The *Chamber of Commerce and* the *Rotarians* have abandoned *their* efforts to re-zone the township.

14 C Use a singular pronoun with two or more singular antecedents joined by *or* or *nor*.

Either Alice *or* Mary may leave *her* children with us.

When one of the antecedents joined by *or* or *nor* is plural, the pronoun must agree with the nearer. (See Sec. 13E.)

Neither the producer nor the *sponsors* admit that *they were* aware of the fraudulent practices. [*They* agrees with the nearer antecedent, *sponsors*.]

Neither the sponsors nor the *producer* admits that *he* was aware of the fraudulent practices. [*He* agrees with the nearer antecedent, *producer*.]

14 D Use a singular pronoun with a collective noun that designates a group as a whole.

The *staff* expressed *its* confidence in the medical director. [The staff acted as a group.]

The *committee* submits *its* report on good and welfare semi-annually. [The committee acts as a group.]

Use a plural pronoun if the collective noun designates the individual members of a group. (See Sec. 13H)

The *staff* have been airing *their* grievances publicly. [Individual members of the staff have been complaining.]

He ordered the *committee* to cease *their* bickering and to attempt to reach an agreement. [Individual members of the committee have been quarreling with each other.]

14 E Use pronouns appropriate in gender to their antecedents.

A masculine pronoun is used with an antecedent denoting a male, a feminine pronoun with an antecedent denoting a female, and a neuter pronoun with all other antecedents.

> The *boxer* was proud of *his* record.
>
> *Mary* resigned from *her* job.
>
> This *comb* has lost most of *its* teeth.

However, feminine pronouns are sometimes used to refer to ships, nations, colleges, and other inanimate things. Masculine pronouns are used with antecedents denoting both sexes. Neuter pronouns are used when the sex is unknown or not specified.

The *Titanic* sank on *her maiden* voyage. [The feminine pronoun is used with the name of a ship.]

Everyone at the meeting expressed *his* indignation. [*His* refers to both the men and women present.]

The native hunters tracked the animal to *its* lair. [The neuter pronoun is used because the sex of the animal is unknown.]

15 REFERENCE OF PRONOUNS

A pronoun is a word that is used in place of a noun. By itself a pronoun is meaningless; a pronoun has meaning only when it refers unmistakably to a noun or pronoun and means the same thing. Consider the following sentences:

She wanted to use *it,* but *it* was broken.

She wanted to use the *eggbeater,* but *it* was broken.

In the first sentence the pronoun *it* could refer to any object, and hence it means nothing. The reader does not know what object she wanted to use only to find broken. In the second sentence, however, the pronoun *it* clearly refers to *eggbeater* and means *eggbeater;* it was the eggbeater she wanted to use, only to find broken.

For this reason the antecedent must be clearly stated, and the pronoun must refer to it unmistakably. Otherwise the reader cannot know what the writer is talking about. The use of the pronouns must therefore meet the following requirements:

1. The pronoun must refer to a stated antecedent.
2. The antecedent must be a noun. The pronoun is a substitute for a noun, not for any other part of speech, nor a phrase, nor a clause, nor a sentence, nor an idea, either expressed or unexpressed.
3. The pronoun must not seem to refer to two or more different antecedents.
4. The pronoun and its antecedent must be close enough for the reader to relate them readily.

15 A Avoid ambiguous reference by making the pronoun refer clearly to only one antecedent.

When a pronoun seems to refer to more than one antecedent, the reference is ambiguous. This kind of obscurity can be avoided in the following ways:

(1) by placing the pronoun close to its antecedent

(2) by repeating the antecedent instead of using the pronoun

(3) by changing indirect statement to direct statement

AMBIGUOUS The captain told the lieutenant that he had unwittingly exceeded his authority. [*Who* had exceeded *whose* authority?]

UNDESIRABLE The captain told the lieutenant that he (the lieutenant) had unwittingly exceeded his authority. [The parenthetical explanation is an admission of inability to write a clear statement.]

CLEAR The captain said to the lieutenant: "You have unwittingly exceeded your authority." [The sentence has been changed from indirect to direct statement.]

AMBIGUOUS Everybody could see that he was a patient who looked closely. [*Who* looked closely? The patient?]

CLEAR Everybody who looked closely could see that he was a patient. [*Who looked closely* has been placed next to *everybody*, the word that it modifies.]

AMBIGUOUS In the attic he found several textbooks with many illustrations which were old. [*Which* were old? The illustrations or the textbooks?]

CLEAR In the attic he found several old textbooks, each with many illustrations. [The sentence has been recast to eliminate the dependent clause *which were old*. *Old* and *each* now clearly modify *textbooks*.]

15 B   Avoid ambiguous reference by making the pronoun refer to a definite antecedent.

General reference, the use of the pronoun to refer to a whole idea or statement, causes obscurity. Most errors of general reference occur with the use of *this, that, which,* and *it.*

OBSCURE   She was practicing a passage of *"Fur Elise"* over and over again, and *it* made him nervous. [*It* refers to the whole idea.]

A faulty reference of this kind should be corrected by revising the sentence to eliminate the pronoun, or by giving the pronoun a definite antecedent. When the pronoun refers to a general idea expressed in the preceding clause, the general idea may be summed up by a noun like *fact, process, act, circumstance, matter* and the like, preceded by *this, that,* and *which.*

CLEAR   She practiced a passage of *"Fur Elise"* over and over again, and *this repetition* made him nervous. [*It* has been replaced by the noun *repetition.*]

OBSCURE   When we arrived at the theatre, John was already there, *which* surprised us greatly. [*Which* has no antecedent.]

CLEAR   When we arrived at the theatre, John was already there. His promptness surprised us greatly. [*Which* has been replaced by *promptness.*]

CLEAR   We were greatly surprised that John was already at the theatre when we arrived.

OBSCURE   Instead of setting a total fee, the orthodontist charged twenty dollars a month until the work was completed, which the dental profession considers unethical. [*Which* does not refer to a definite antecedent.]

CLEAR   Instead of setting a total fee, the orthodontist charged twenty dollars a month until the work was finished, an arrangement which the dental profession considers unethical. [*Which* now refers to the antecedent *arrangement*, a noun which sums up the general idea expressed in the previous clause.]

15 C Avoid indefinite or implied reference by making the pronoun refer to a definite antecedent.

Do not use a pronoun to refer to a word that has been implied, but not expressed. The reader must not be asked to guess the antecedent or to supply it by inference.

IMPLIED REFERENCE   My father wants me to be a doctor, but this is a profession that does not appeal to me. [*This* has no antecedent.]

CLEAR   My father wants me to be a doctor, but *medicine* is a profession that does not appeal to me.

IMPLIED REFERENCE   I have visited Benson College, but I do not want to go there because they are snobs? [*Who* are snobs? *They* has no antecedent.]

CLEAR   I have visited Benson College, but I do not want to go there because *the students* are snobs.

15 D Avoid remote reference by placing the antecedent in an emphatic position in the sentence.

If the antecedent of a pronoun is in a subordinate construction, or if it is widely separated from the pronoun, the reference of the pronoun may be vague. This kind of obscurity can be avoided by repeating the antecedent or by putting it in a more prominent position in the sentence.

VAGUE   James Joyce's *Dubliners* is a collection of short stories about the moral life of Dublin. *He* was a native of Dublin and knew intimately the life of the city. [*He* refers to a remote antecedent, *James Joyce's,* which is a possessive adjective instead of a noun.]

CLEAR   James Joyce's *Dubliners* is a collection of short stories about the moral life of Dublin. *Joyce* was a native of Dublin and knew the life of the city intimately. [The noun *Joyce* is substituted for the pronoun.]

VAGUE   While bathing in the surf at Malibu Beach, he was knocked down and almost drowned. *It* was too strong for him to breast. [The antecedent *surf* is remote from *it,* and *Malibu Beach* intervenes.]

CLEAR   While bathing in the surf at Malibu Beach, he was knocked down and almost drowned. The *surf* was too strong for him to breast. [The pronoun *it* has been replaced by the antecedent *surf.*]

15 E   Do not use *same, said,* and *such* instead of *this, that,* and *it.*

JARGON   Everybody thought that the will had been lost, but *said* document was found in an old safe.

IMPROVED   Everybody thought that the will had been lost, but *it* (or *this document*) was found in an old safe.

JARGON   I have received your manuscript and read *same* very carefully.

IMPROVED   I have received your manuscript and read *it* very carefully.

15 F Avoid anticipatory reference by expressing the antecedent before referring to it with a pronoun.

Anticipatory reference, a reference in which the pronoun precedes the antecedent, is usually awkward and confusing. It keeps the reader uninformed for too long a time and may cause him to lose part of the thought. Except in short sentences, the antecedent should, as its name implies, precede the pronoun.

OBSCURE   If they are washed gently with warm water and a mild detergent and are then wrapped in a soft, absorbent cloth and left to dry, these *orlon garments* will retain their original shape and texture.

CLEAR   If these *orlon garments* are washed with warm water and a mild detergent and are then wrapped in a soft, absorbent cloth and left to dry, *they* will retain their original shape and texture.

ACCEPTABLE   When I received *it*, the *shirt* was stained.

BETTER   When I received the *shirt*, it was *stained*.

16 CASE

Case denotes the relation of nouns and pronouns to other words in the sentence. There are three relationships or cases:

(1) The nominative case indicates that the noun or pronoun is used as the subject of a verb, or as an appositive to a subject noun, or as a predicate noun.

Mary plays the piano. [Nominative case, subject of the verb.]

The younger *girl, Mary,* plays the piano. [*Mary* is in the nominative case as the appositive to *girl*.]

The girl playing the piano is *Mary*. [*Mary* is in the nominative case because it is a predicate noun used after the copulative verb *is* to refer to *girl*.]

(2) The possessive case indicates possession.

I tuned *Mary's* piano.

(3) The objective case indicates that the noun or pronoun receives the action of the verb or the verbal, or that it is the object of a preposition.

I tuned the *piano*. [Object of *tuned*]

Tuning the *piano* was easy. [Object of the gerund *tuning*]

She sat down at the *piano* to play. [Object of the preposition *at*]

As these illustrations show, nouns and pronouns indicate case either by their position in the sentence or by their form. Nouns retain the same form in the nominative and objective cases, but change form to indicate the possessive case: *Mary's*. The personal pronouns, except *you* and *it*, have different forms for the nominative and objective cases as well as for the possessive case. (*I, mine, me; he, his, him; she, hers, her; you, your, yours; it, its.*)

Since the improper use of case brands the writer as semi-literate and may result in obscurity, the writer must learn to use nouns and pronouns in their proper case. Nouns cause little trouble because they change form only in the possessive case. The personal pronouns, however, cause some writers considerable difficulty and must therefore be used with special care.

16 A   Put the subject of a verb in the nominative case.

John is growing taller.

He was born in Vernal, Colorado.

They are studying nuclear physics.

16 B   Put a predicate noun or pronoun in the nominative case.

The predicate noun or pronoun stands for the same person or thing as the subject and renames it. Therefore the predicate noun or pronoun is in the same case as the subject, the nominative case.

> Mr. Dill is a *sexton*.
>
> It was *he* who wrote the letter.
>
> They thought that the thief was *I*.

16 C   Put the appositive of a subject in the nominative case.

Mr. Daly, my *neighbor*, is a probation officer.

The sponsors, *we who are present here*, must sign the petition.

16 D   Put the object of a verb in the objective case.

> He blew the *whistle*.
>
> We thanked *him* for his kindness.
>
> He taught *her* Greek.

16 E   Put the object or complement of a verbal in the objective case.

Smelling the *coffee*, I jumped out of bed. [*Coffee* is the object of the participle *smelling*.]

Whipping *him* does no good. [*Him* is the object of the gerund *whipping*.]

I should like to be *him*. [*Him* is the predicate complement of the infinitive *to be*.]

16 F   Put the subject of an infinitive in the objective case.

We asked *him* to be our representative. [*Him* is the subject of the infinitive *to be*.]

We hired *her* to demonstrate our products. [*Her* is the subject of the infinitive *to demonstrate*.]

16 G   Put coordinate nouns and pronouns in the same case.

Mr. Sahn and *I* are on the nominating committee. [*Mr. Sahn* and *I* are subjects of the verb and are therefore in the nominative case.]

He reported *Jones* and *me* to the supervisor. [As objects of *reported, Jones* and *me* are in the objective case.]

16 H   In all elliptical clauses introduced by *than* and *as* put nouns and pronouns in the case which the expanded clause would demand.

He received the appointment because he has more experience than *I* [*have*].

Mr. Anderson did not recommend him as highly as [he recommended] *me*.

16 I   Put the object of a preposition in the objective case.

Grandmother's linens will be divided between *you* and *me*. [*You* and *me* are objects of the preposition *between*.]

We will divide the spoils among *us*. [*Us* is the object of the preposition *among*.]

16 J
Put the relative pronoun *who* or *whom* in the case demanded by its use in the clause to which it belongs.

Livingston was the man *who* was sent to find Stanley. [*Who* introduces the dependent clause and is the nominative case because it is the subject of the verb *was*.]

Who do you suppose gave him our address? [*Who* is the subject of *gave*, not the object of the parenthetical clause *do you suppose*.]

Whom were they talking about? [*Whom* is the object of the preposition *about*.]

Whom do you take them to be? [*Whom* is the complement of the infinitive *to be*.]

Help *whoever* deserves help. [*Whoever* is the subject of the verb *deserves* and is therefore in the nominative case.]

16 K
Put nouns and pronouns in the possessive case when they are used to show the following:

(1) Possession

Mary's doll [the doll that Mary owns]

his kite

(2) Connection

China's apologists [apologists who represent China]

the bureau's legal advisors

(3) The performer of an act

Houdini's escape [Houdini *did* escape.]

the King's abdication

(4) Time, measurement, weight

      a day's wages [the wages earned in a day]

      a hair's breadth [the width of a hair]

16 L   Put a noun or pronoun in the possessive case when it *immediately* precedes a gerund.

Whenever she thinks of *Henry's leaving*, she begins to cry.

I will not take the blame for *somebody's pilfering*.

He slipped away without *anybody's noticing* him. [Compare this illustration with the next.]

He slipped away without *anybody* in the room *noticing* him. [Here the possessive case of *anybody* is not used because it does not *immediately* precede the gerund.]

NOTE: A noun preceding a participle is not in the possessive case.

The *girl singing* in the next room is my sister. [*Singing in the next room* is a participial phrase used as an adjective to modify *girl*, the subject of the verb *is*.]

The *girl's singing* of Brahms' "Lullaby" was musical. [*Singing* is a gerund, the subject of the verb *was*. *Girl's* is the possessive case because it immediately precedes the gerund *singing*.]

17 DANGLING MODIFIERS

A dangling modifier is a dependent construction which is related to the wrong word in the sentence. As a result the sentence is momentarily misleading and frequently ludicrous.

Coming around the bend in the road, the church was seen. In this sentence the participial phrase *coming around the bend in the road* modifies *church* and makes the ludicrous assertion that the church was coming around the bend. The phrase *coming around the bend in the road* logically modifies a noun or pronoun that is not expressed in the sentence.

Coming around the bend in the road, we saw a church. In the revised sentence the participial phrase is correctly used because it modifies *we,* and *we* can logically come around the bend and see a church. A modifier dangles, therefore, when it modifies a word that cannot logically perform the action which the modifier expresses.

17 A Avoid dangling participial and gerund phrases.

DANGLING   *Looking through my field glasses,* the bird flew away. [The phrase dangles because it ludicrously modifies *bird.*]

CORRECT   *Looking through my field glasses, I* saw the bird fly away. [The sentence has been changed from the passive to the active voice, and the phrase does not dangle because it logically modifies the pronoun *I.*]

DANGLING   The visitors watched the construction men at work in the excavation, *gaping in open-mouthed wonder.* [The phrase dangles because it does not clearly modify *visitors* and illogically seems to modify either *excavation* or *men.*]

CORRECT   *Gaping in open-mouthed wonder, the visitors* watched the construction men at work in the excavation. [The phrase now immediately precedes *visitors* and correctly modifies it.]

DANGLING   *On examining his account,* the discrepancy became apparent. [The phrase is incorrectly related to *discrepancy.* Did the *discrepancy* examine?]

CORRECT *On examining his account, he* discovered the discrepancy. [The phrase is now correctly related to *he*.]

To test for dangling participial and gerund phrases, ask the question: can the subject of the independent clause do what the phrase says is being done? If not, the phrase dangles. The following sentences show the usefulness of this test.

Growling and straining at the leash, I was frightened by the dog. [Was *I* growling and straining at the leash?]

Attempting to tune the violin, the "G" string broke. [Was the *"G" string* attempting to tune the violin?]

The boy's shoes are always scraped by *climbing trees* and *crawling on the ground.* [Do shoes or trees climb and crawl?]

A writer can easily avoid many dangling introductory phrases by observing the following rule: An introductory gerund or participial phrase should be followed immediately by the word it modifies.

Attempting to tune the violin, *the teacher* . . .

Growling and straining at the leash, *the dog* . . .

Lowering the shades, *she* . . .

Believing that he would receive bipartisan support, *the President* . . .

17 B Avoid dangling infinitive phrases.

Like participial and gerund phrases, infinitive phrases dangle when they are related to the wrong word in the sentence. In general, the rules for detecting and avoiding dangling gerund and participial phrases also apply to dangling infinitive phrases.

DANGLING *To provide maximum coverage, you* must have a comprehensive policy. [*You* do not provide the coverage.]

CORRECT *To provide maximum coverage, a policy* must be comprehensive. [The *policy* provides the coverage.]

DANGLING *To bake a delicious cake, the eggs and butter* must be fresh. [Do *eggs and butter* bake a cake?]

CORRECT *To bake a delicious cake, you* must use fresh eggs and butter. [*You* can bake a cake.]

DANGLING The flight was too dangerous to attempt. [*To attempt* can be related only to *dangerous* or to *flight,* neither of which can *attempt.*]

CORRECT This flight is too dangerous *for us* to attempt. [*To attempt* is now logically related to *us.*]

17 C   Avoid dangling elliptical clauses and phrases.

An elliptical clause or phrase is one from which words have been omitted because the reader will readily supply them. The following elliptical constructions are correct:

My sister is older than I [am].

When [you are] learning to type, you should not look at the keys.

A dangling elliptical construction is one that invites the reader to complete it with words that mislead him or produce a ludicrous effect. The writer can correct this error by expanding the elliptical construction or by supplying the word to which it should properly relate.

DANGLING *When eight years old, my father* began to teach me Greek. [Father was eight years old?]

CORRECT — When *I* was eight years old, *my father* began to teach me Greek. [The elliptical clause has been expanded.]

DANGLING — *When thoroughly cleaned, you* should wash the fish and salt it lightly. [When *you* are thoroughly cleaned?]

CORRECT — *When you have thoroughly cleaned the fish, you* should wash it and salt it lightly. [The elliptical clause has been expanded by the addition of the missing subject and object.]

17 D   Do not confuse participles with certain prepositions and prepositional phrases.

Words and phrases like *allowing, granting, assuming, according to, relating to, rejecting, concerning, speaking of, considering, owing to*, etc. are used as prepositions and are therefore not regarded as dangling modifiers.

Owing to certain technical difficulties, the program announced for this time will not be broadcast.

Considering the large amount of advertising, the increase in sales has been disappointing.

18   THE POSITION OF MODIFIERS

The meaning of an English sentence is largely dependent on the position of its parts. Therefore, a modifying word, phrase, or clause must be so placed in a sentence that the reader immediately connects it with the word that it modifies. A modifier is properly placed when (1) it is next to or close to the word that it modifies and when (2) it is not near another word that it can mistakenly modify.

18 A Place the adverbs *only*, *almost*, *ever*, *merely*, *scarcely*, *just*, and *even* next to the word they modify.

In colloquial writing and speaking these adverbs may be carelessly placed, but in formal writing they should be carefully placed in their logical position.

COLLOQUIAL   He *merely* asked the question because he was curious.

FORMAL   He asked the question *merely* because he was curious.

COLLOQUIAL   She *almost* washed the whole set of dishes.

FORMAL   She washed *almost* the whole set of dishes.

18 B Place a phrase so that it is clearly related to the word that it logically modifies.

AMBIGUOUS   He offered to paint the fence *last night*.

CLEAR   *Last night* he offered to paint the fence.

AMBIGUOUS   He was bored by the charades and wished that he had not come *after an hour*.

CLEAR   *After an hour* he was bored by the charades and wished that he had not come.

18 C Place a dependent clause so that it is clearly related to the word that it logically modifies.

AMBIGUOUS   He finally got rid of his hiccoughs by holding his breath *which had lasted an hour*.

CLEAR   By holding his breath, he finally got rid of his hiccoughs *which had lasted an hour*.

AMBIGUOUS   In his last years Grandfather told me about the pioneer days in the West and about prospecting for gold in Alaska *in a way that I will never forget.*

CLEAR   In his last years Grandfather told me, *in a way that I will never forget,* about the pioneer days in the West and about prospecting for gold in Alaska.

18 D   **Do not place a modifier where it seems to modify either the preceding or the following words.**

This kind of modifier is sometimes called a squinting modifier because it points in two directions at the same time.

AMBIGUOUS   The doctor said that if he did not move to a warmer clime *within a year* he would be dead. [Must he *move* within a year, or will he be *dead* within a year?]

CLEAR   The doctor said that if he did not move to a warmer clime he would be dead *within a year.*

AMBIGUOUS   While we were dining in Flagstaff, Arizona, *on the advice of a fellow traveler* we decided to see Boulder Dam. [What did we do on advice, dine or decide to see Boulder Dam?]

CLEAR   While we were dining in Flagstaff, Arizona, we decided, *on the advice of a fellow traveler,* to see Boulder Dam.

19 SPLIT AND MIXED CONSTRUCTIONS

The related words of a sentence belong together. The pointless separation of closely related words often causes awkwardness or obscurity. When separation produces either of these effects, the writer should change the order of the words or revise the sentence.

19 A   Avoid split infinitives.

The infinitive is regarded as a unit and normally should not be split by the insertion of an adverb, e.g., *to rapidly advance*. However, an infinitive may sometimes be split in order to avoid awkwardness or to achieve emphasis. Generally speaking, the writer should avoid splitting an infinitive and should use a split infinitive only if it makes a sentence smoother, clear, or more emphatic.

AWKWARD   I am unable *to honestly say* that I like sheath dresses.

IMPROVED   I am unable *to say honestly* that I like sheath dresses.

AWKWARD   You must now begin *to, if you have the time, read* more widely in the literature of psychology.

IMPROVED   If you now have the time, you must begin *to read* more widely in the literature of psychology.

JUSTIFIED   I hope that you will be able *to satisfactorily repair* my television set within a week. [Putting *satisfactorily* either before or after *to repair* would make the sentence awkward and misleading.]

19 B   Avoid the aimless separation of verb and object.

AWKWARD   He acknowledged, with a little bow, the compliment.

IMPROVED With a little bow he acknowledged the compliment.

AWKWARD Looking through his binoculars, he saw on the opposite shore a group of bathers.

IMPROVED Looking through his binoculars, he saw a group of bathers on the opposite shore.

19 C Avoid the aimless separation of preposition and object.

AWKWARD She pawed through every garment on the bargain counter, looking for, in that welter, a small blouse.

IMPROVED She pawed through every garment on the bargain counter, looking for a small blouse in that welter.

AWKWARD He would arrive at the lake on Tuesday or Wednesday, depending on, he said, the amount of work to be finished at the office.

IMPROVED He would arrive at the lake on Tuesday or Wednesday, depending, he said, on the amount of work to be finished at the office.

19 D Avoid the aimless separation of a reference word and its antecedent.

AWKWARD He was most impressed by the *applicant,* as I fully expected, *whom* his brother-in-law recommended.

IMPROVED He was most impressed, as I fully expected, by the *applicant whom* his brother-in-law recommended.

AWKWARD He wanted to discharge *everyone* at once *who* took part in the work stoppage. [Separation of a *who* clause and its antecedent, *everyone.*]

IMPROVED   He wanted to discharge at once *everyone who* took part in the work stoppage.

19 E   Avoid the aimless separation of the parts of a verb phrase.

AWKWARD   There stands the house that I *will,* within five years, *purchase and remodel.*

IMPROVED   There stands the house that I *will purchase and remodel* within five years.

AWKWARD   They feared that she *was* now, after the birth of her child, *reconsidering* her decision to place it for adoption.

IMPROVED   They feared that now, after the birth of her child, she *was reconsidering* her decision to place it for adoption.

19 F   Avoid the aimless separation of coordinate or parallel parts of a sentence.

AWKWARD   *After we had signed the contract,* we took possession of the house *after we had made the initial payment.* [The coordinate adverbial clauses are needlessly separated.]

IMPROVED   *After we had signed the contract and made the initial payment,* we took possession of the house.

AWKWARD   *The men removed their hats* when Her Majesty appeared on the balcony *and the ladies cheered.*

IMPROVED   *The men removed their hats, and the ladies cheered* when Her Majesty appeared on the balcony.

19 G   Avoid mixed constructions.

A mixed construction is a blend of two different constructions in one sentence. The writer should not begin a sentence with one construction and end with another. The blending or confusion of different constructions within a sentence results in awkwardness and obscurity.

MIXED
There is no one to whom he can apply to for help. [This sentence is a blend of *There is no one to whom he can apply for help* and *There is no one whom he can apply to for help.*]

MIXED
I *urged* him to invest in mutual funds if he *can.* [The tenses of the verbs in direct and indirect discourse are confused.]

IMPROVED
I urged him, "Invest in mutual funds if you *can.*" [Direct statement]

IMPROVED
I urged him to invest in mutual funds if he *could.* [Indirect statement]

MIXED
He asked me would I drive him to town. [Here an infinitive construction is confused with a clause.]

IMPROVED
He asked me to drive him to town. [The infinitive *to drive* is used as the complement of *asked.*]

IMPROVED
He asked me if I would drive him to town. [A clause is used as the complement of *asked.*]

MIXED
In order to complete the installation before the end of the month is why we are working overtime. [The construction shifts and makes the introductory adverbial phrase the subject of the sentence.]

IMPROVED In order to complete the installation before the end of the month, we are working overtime. [*We* is now the subject of *are working*, a verb phrase which is properly modified by the introductory adverbial phrase.]

IMPROVED The reason why we are working overtime is to complete the installation before the end of the month. [Here the introductory clause is the subject of *is*.]

MIXED The company repudiated the agreement which, although it made several concessions to the union, the terms seemed to be to its advantage. [Before one construction is completed the sentence shifts to another, leaving *which* without a predicate.]

IMPROVED The company repudiated the agreement which, although it made several concessions to the union, seemed to be to its advantage. [*Which* is now the subject of *seemed*.]

MIXED Agencies must figure out how many people will the advertisement reach. [This is a blend of a declarative and interrogative sentence.]

IMPROVED Agencies must figure out how many people the advertisement will reach. [Placing *will* in its proper place makes this a declarative sentence.]

Must the agencies figure out how many people the advertisement will reach? [Interrogative sentence]

MIXED What he forgot to consider was would he break a limb on the ski jump. [A blend of a declarative and interrogative sentence.]

IMPROVED   What he forgot to consider was the possibility of breaking a limb on the ski jump. [A declarative sentence] Did he forget to consider the possibility that he might break a limb on the ski jump? [An interrogative sentence]

20 INCOMPLETE COMPARISONS

In written English, comparisons should be logical and complete. Incomplete comparisons are illogical and misleading. The writer should express both terms of the comparison and include all of the words necessary to make clear the relationship between the terms.

20 A Do not omit *than* or *as* in a double comparison.

INCOMPLETE   He is as wealthy, if not wealthier than, his uncle.

COMPLETE   He is as wealthy as his uncle, if not wealthier.

INCOMPLETE   In percentage, wages have increased as much, if not more than prices.

COMPLETE   In percentage, wages have increased as much as prices, if not more.

NOTE: Although some writers use the suspended construction, many others object to its awkwardness. The suspended construction can easily be avoided.

SUSPENDED   In the ring, Tag Martin is as ferocious as, if not more ferocious than Jack Dempsey was.

IMPROVED   In the ring, Tag Martin is as ferocious as Jack Dempsey was, if not more ferocious.

20 B   Do not omit *other* after *than* or *as* when comparing two members of the same class.

ILLOGICAL   Alaska is bigger than any state in the union. [Is Alaska bigger than itself?]

LOGICAL   Alaska is bigger than any *other* state in the union.

ILLOGICAL   Jefferson was more cultured than any of the founding fathers. [Was not Jefferson a founding father?]

LOGICAL   Jefferson was more cultured than any of the *other* founding fathers.

20 C   Do not omit one term of a comparison.

AMBIGUOUS   I rank Gilbert and Sullivan higher than Rodgers and Hammerstein. [Higher than Rodgers and Hammerstein rank Gilbert and Sullivan?]

IMPROVED   I rank Gilbert and Sullivan higher than I *rank* Rodgers and Hammerstein.

AMBIGUOUS   Shaw liked Wagner better than Verdi. [Better than Shaw liked Verdi, or than Verdi liked Wagner?]

IMPROVED   Shaw liked Wagner better than *he liked* Verdi.

IMPROVED   Shaw liked Wagner better than *Verdi liked* him.

20 D   Do not compare things which are not consistent or capable of being compared.

ILLOGICAL   The mountains in Vermont are lower and greener than New Hampshire. [Mountains cannot be compared to a state.]

LOGICAL   The mountains in Vermont are lower and greener than *the mountains* in New Hampshire. [Mountains are compared to mountains.]

ILLOGICAL   The filter in Superbas removes more tars and nicotine than any other cigarette. [A filter cannot be compared to a cigarette.]

LOGICAL   The filter in Superbas removes more tars and nicotine than the filter of any other cigarette. [Filter is now compared to filter.]

20 E   Do not use the following phrases inexactly: *than any, than any other, of all, of any, all else, of all others.*

ILLOGICAL   He is reputed to be the most skillful of any politician in the state. [The superlative *most skillful* refers to one of three or more things and cannot logically be used with the singular *any.*]

LOGICAL   He is reputed to be the most skillful politician in the state.

ILLOGICAL   I like the *Times* best of all the city's other papers. [*Other* must not be used after the superlative *best, most,* etc.]

LOGICAL   I like the *Times* best of all the city's papers.

ILLOGICAL   Shakespeare is better than any English poet. [Was not Shakespeare an English poet?]

LOGICAL   Shakespeare is better than any *other* English poet.

20 F   Do not use *any* in an *of* phrase following a superlative.

ILLOGICAL   He is the best of *any* popular singer now appearing on television.

LOGICAL   He is the best of all popular singers now appearing on television.

ILLOGICAL   This machine is the most efficient of *any* typewriter now on the market.

LOGICAL   This machine is the most efficient typewriter now on the market. OR This machine is the most efficient *of all* the typewriters now on the market.

20 G **Do not use the comparative form to compare more than two terms; do not use the superlative form to compare fewer than three terms.**

INCORRECT   She is the *prettiest* of the twins.

CORRECT   She is the *prettier* of the twins.

INCORRECT   I am the *older* of *three* brothers.

CORRECT   I am the *oldest* of *three* brothers.

21 OMISSION OF NECESSARY WORDS

The writer should be careful to include every word that is necessary to the meaning of the sentence. The omission of necessary words may cause awkwardness or obscurity.

21 A Do not write a telegraphic style.

A telegraphic style should be used only in telegrams, cook books, and other manuals of instruction, diaries, etc.

TELEGRAPHIC   Reported late to work this morning because of accident.

IMPROVED   I reported late to work this morning because of a slight accident.

21 B Do not omit the necessary article in coordinate and parallel forms.

CORRECT   He waved a red and blue flag. [He waved one flag combining two colors.]

CORRECT   He waved a red and *a* blue flag. [He waved two different flags.]

CORRECT   When he appeared for the hearing he was accompanied by a friend and advisor. [The friend and advisor is one person.]

CORRECT   When he appeared for the hearing, he was accompanied by a friend and *an* advisor. [The friend and the advisor are two different people.]

21 C Do not omit necessary pronouns.

MISLEADING   She is always accompanied by her young niece and companion. [Is the niece her companion also?]

IMPROVED   She is always accompanied by her young niece and *her* companion. [The repetition of *her* shows that she was accompanied by two people.]

MISLEADING   From his income tax he deducted the expenses for his office and showroom. [Was the office and showroom one place?]

IMPROVED   From his income tax he deducted the expenses for his office and *his* showroom. [The repetition of *his* shows that the office and the showroom are two different places.]

21 D Do not omit necessary prepositions.

INCOMPLETE   He has never expressed trust or loyalty to anyone. [*In* is omitted after *trust*.]

COMPLETE   He has never expressed trust in or loyalty to anyone.

INCOMPLETE   He has stored his equipment in the cellar and the attic. [*In* is ommited before *the attic*.]

COMPLETE   He has stored his equipment in the cellar and *in* the attic.

21 E Do not omit part of a verb phrase requiring a different form from that of the accompanying verb phrase.

INCOMPLETE   He always has and always will be inconsiderate. [*Be* is the correct form after *will*, but not after *has*.]

COMPLETE   He always *has been* and always *will be* inconsiderate. [*Been* is the proper form after has; *be* is proper after *will*.]

INCOMPLETE   I have received many of his books and will the others. [*Received* is the proper form after *have*, but not after *will*.]

COMPLETE   I have received many of his books and will receive the others. [*Received* is the proper form after *have*; *receive* is proper after *will*.]

21 F Do not omit a necessary *is* or *was* from a verb phrase.

INCOMPLETE   She is charming and loved by everyone. [*Is* must be repeated to complete the verb phrase *is loved*.]

COMPLETE She is charming and is loved by everyone.

INCOMPLETE He was late for work and reprimanded by the supervisor. [*Was* must be repeated to complete the verb phrase *was reprimanded*.]

COMPLETE He was late for work and *was* reprimanded by the supervisor.

21 G **Do not omit the verb after a subject requiring a different verb from that of the preceding subject.**

INCOMPLETE The material is sturdy and the buttons beautiful. [The singular *is* is correct after the singular *material*, but not after the plural subject, *buttons*.]

COMPLETE The material is sturdy, and the buttons *are* beautiful. [The plural form *are* has been inserted after the plural subject *buttons*.]

INCOMPLETE His manner was offensive and his reasons lame. [The singular *was* is correct after *manner*, but not after *reasons*.]

COMPLETE His manner *was* offensive, and his reasons *were* lame.

21 H **Do not omit *that* after verbs of saying, thinking, hoping, feeling, wishing, etc.**

INCOMPLETE He impatiently replied he was well aware of the situation. [This sentence seems to be a fusion of two sentences.]

COMPLETE He impatiently replied *that* he was well aware of the situation. [The relative pronoun *that* properly relates the dependent clause to the independent clause.]

INCOMPLETE   The villain softly murmured with a fervent
              sigh she was breaking his heart. [This sen-
              tence seems to be a fusion of two sentences.]

COMPLETE   The villain softly murmured with a fervent
              sigh *that* she was breaking his heart.

21 I   Do not omit *much* after *very* in a passive verb phrase.

INCOMPLETE   The president was very pleased with the ac-
              countant's suggestion.

COMPLETE   The president was very *much* pleased with the
              accountant's suggestion.

INCOMPLETE   I was very satisfied with the results of the
              campaign.

COMPLETE   I was very *much* satisfied with the results of
              the campaign.

21 J   Do not omit words necessary to make a parallel series intelligible

INCOMPLETE   The house is about fifty years old, sprawling,
              very ugly, and falling apart.

COMPLETE   The house is about fifty years old. It is
              sprawling and ugly and is falling apart.

INCOMPLETE   Shallow, muddy, full of weeds, good only for
              fishing, the lake cannot be developed as a
              summer resort.

COMPLETE   Shallow, muddy, and full of weeds, the lake
              is good only for fishing. It cannot be devel-
              oped as a summer resort.

21 K   Do not use *so*, *such*, and *too* as exclamations.

These words should be followed by a phrase or a clause.

INCOMPLETE   Her new coat is too beautiful! [Too beautiful for what?]

COMPLETE   Her new coat is too beautiful to wear to work.

COMPLETE   Her coat is very beautiful.

INCOMPLETE   He is so docile! [So docile that what?]

COMPLETE   He is so docile that everybody takes advantage of him.

COMPLETE   He is unusually docile.

· EMPHASIS, CONSISTENCY, AND APPROPRIATENESS

22 EMPHASIS

It is frequently desirable to emphasize an entire sentence, or a single word or a group of words within a sentence. Without the use of emphasis, writing is flat and uninteresting.

22A EMPHASIS BY ARRANGEMENT

To give prominence to an entire sentence, place it either at the beginning or end of the paragraph. The beginning of a paragraph calls attention to itself simply because it is the first thing to engage the reader's attention. The end of a paragraph can be made prominent by building the previous sentences to a climax, or by arranging them in an order of ascending importance so that the thought expressed by the concluding sentence is given added forcefulness by what precedes it.

The roads were hot and dusty. The grass in the meadows was burned to a parched golden brown. Cattle in dried up river bottoms licked hopefully at gravel and rocks where water had always been before. *It had not rained for weeks, and there would be no rain for two more weeks to come.*

To give emphasis to single words or groups of words, pay attention to the arrangement of the order of the words as they occur in the sentence. Words at the beginning and end of a sentence are likely to attract more attention than words in the middle. Words or phrases placed out of their usual or expected positions also call attention to themselves. Careful use of these general principles—avoiding the abuse of straining too hard or too frequently for special effects—is a large part of the secret of varied and effective writing.

In normal English word order, for example, adjectives precede the nouns they modify. Reversing this order calls particular attention to the adjectives.

NORMAL: The *tired old* judge slumped on the bench.

REVERSED: The judge, *old* and *tired,* slumped on the bench.

This procedure cannot be used for a single adjective without producing an overly artificial effect: *The judge, old, slumped on the bench.*

In normal word order the flow of a sentence moves from the subject to the verb and concludes with words related to the verb (as complements or modifiers).

The captain led his men into battle. [object *men* and modifier *into battle*]

The young man walked *rapidly down the street because he was anxious to get home.* [adverbial modifiers after verb]

The only exception occurs when the sentence is introduced by the expletive *here* or *there: There were forty men in the room.*

The following sentence represents the usual flow of words:

John and Barbara were married on a sunny afternoon in late November.

[subject]   [verb]   [adverbial modifiers]

The statement is clear, but no part of it is emphasized because the order of the words is exactly what the reader expects. To give prominence to adverbial modifiers, place them at the beginning of the sentence. To emphasize the date, recast the sentence to read:

In late November, John and Barbara were married on a sunny afternoon.

To emphasize both the weather and the date, revise the sentence to read:

On a sunny afternoon in late November, John and Barbara were married.

Observe particularly how placing the adverbial modifiers (*on a sunny afternoon in late November*) at the beginning of the sentence not only makes them more prominent but also gives greater emphasis to the concluding verb *were married*. Notice, too, how the abnormal word order of this sentence calls attention to the entire sentence and makes it more interesting and emphatic.

The same principle applies to the position of single words in the sentence.

NORMAL: He drew himself to attention smartly.

EMPHATIC: Smartly he drew himself to attention.

To give emphasis to the object of a verb (which normally follows the verb), place the object at the beginning of the sentence.

NORMAL: They made him president.

EMPHATIC: Him they made president.

In some sentences, a telling and dramatic effect can be achieved by completely reversing normal word order.

NORMAL: The men marched into the battle.

REVERSED: Into the battle marched the men.

CAUTION: Do not try to recast every sentence, or even the majority of sentences, to secure emphasis. Such a procedure defeats its own purpose by producing an effect of strained and artificial writing. In the following paragraph, the plight of three boys is described. The writer was principally interested in one of the boys, John. He therefore reserves the description of John's misfortune for the end, and he uses abnormal word order only in the concluding sentence.

> They tied Fred to a tree. They perched Jimmy on top of a high rock. John they threw into the river.

Observe how the beginning and end of a sentence call attention to themselves, particularly when the word order is at all unusual. It follows that, even in the construction of ordinary sentences, it is foolish to place unimportant words or phrases in emphatic positions. In the sentence,

> However, the nurse did not arrive.

the sentence modifier *however* does not deserve the emphasis its position gives it. Revising the sentence to

> The nurse, however, did not arrive.

gives prominence to the essential parts of the statement.

Similarly, unimportant words or phrases at the end of a sentence occupy a position of prominence which would be better held by more important material.

> Thousands of spectators packed the stadium to watch the championship game on Thanksgiving Day.

Unless the date is important in this sentence, it should be inserted within the sentence:

> Thousands of spectators packed the stadium on Thanksgiving Day to watch the championship game.

22 B EMPHASIS BY REPETITION

When a word or phrase is repeated immediately or soon after its original use, the reader is certain to notice the repetition. Deliberate repetition, therefore, is a certain method for obtaining emphasis.

His father was *weak*, his sister was *weak*, and he was *weak*.

. . . that government of the *people*, by the *people*, for the *people* . . .

"Houses of refuge *don't have crews*, said the correspondent. As I understand them, they are only places where clothes and grub are stored for the benefit of shipwrecked people. They *don't carry crews.*"

"Oh, yes, they do," said the cook.

"No, they don't," said the correspondent.

"Well, *we're not there yet*, anyhow," *said the oiler in the stern.*

"Well," said the cook, "perhaps it's not a house of refuge that I'm thinking of as being near Mosquito Inlet Light. Perhaps it's a life-saving station."

"*We're not there yet*," *said the oiler in the stern.*

—Stephen Crane, "The Open Boat"

22 C EMPHASIS BY USE OF VOICE

The choice of active or passive voice (See 3 E) should depend on which element of the sentence is to be emphasized. In a typical sentence containing a transitive verb, such as

John owns a horse.

the use of the active voice emphasizes John's ownership. If the statement is intended to answer a question about the horse, it should be placed in the passive voice:

> The horse is owned by John.

In general, if there is no particular problem of emphasis, the active voice is preferable since it is more direct and gives a stronger effect.

> The members will be notified by the president.

is less emphatic than

> The president will notify the members.

22 D EMPHASIS BY SUBORDINATION

To give a flat and lifeless effect to writing, the simplest device is to use only simple and compound sentences in normal word order. Writers often do this deliberately to create a pallid atmosphere:

> He went into the house. He looked around listlessly for a few minutes and then slumped into a chair. No sound was heard except the ticking of the clock. He rested his head on the back of the chair and gradually fell into a deep and profound sleep.

But to indicate distinctions between ideas of greater and lesser importance, place the lesser words and phrases in subordinate positions in the sentence (as described in 22 A) and place the less important clauses in subordinate form. In the following sentence, nothing is emphasized, and the entire statement is flat:

> New York City is on the East Coast, and it is America's largest seaport.

To stress the location of New York City, recast the sentence as follows:

New York City, which is America's largest seaport, is on the East Coast.

To stress the importance of New York City as a seaport, rewrite the sentence:

New York City, which is on the East Coast, is America's largest seaport.

22 E COORDINATION AND BALANCE

Words and phrases are coordinated by using the coordinating conjunctions *and, but, or, nor, for, yet.*

He was poor *but* happy.

The decor of the lobby was rich, *yet* unobtrusive.

Clauses are coordinated by joining them with a coordinating conjunction or a semicolon.

Ideas of equal importance are given equal prominence by coordination. The elements to be coordinated are given increased emphasis if they are balanced: presented in approximately the same number of words, the same kind of words, and in identical or closely similar word order.

He gained great wealth, but he lost his honor.

To err is human; to forgive, divine.

The man was the hunter; the woman was the cook.

He'll come willingly or he won't come at all.

Balance also gives effectiveness to simple assertions:

Sauce for the goose is sauce for the gander.

Over the fence is out of bounds.

22 F PARALLELISM AND BALANCE

Two or more ideas which are similar in nature are known as parallel ideas. For effective presentation, express them in parallel form: a noun should be paralleled with a noun, an infinitive with an infinitive, a subordinate clause with another subordinate clause, etc.

PARALLEL NOUNS	They studied *history, mathematics,* and *chemistry.*
NOT PARALLEL	They studied about the past, mathematics, and how matter is constituted.
PARALLEL INFINITIVES	He learned *to swim, to play* tennis, and *to ride* a horse.
NOT PARALLEL	He learned to play tennis, swimming, and the art of horseback riding.
PARALLEL CLAUSES	In her praises of the summer camp, she mentioned *that the food was good, that the climate was perfect,* and *that the equipment was superb.*
NOT PARALLEL	In her praises of the summer camp, she mentioned the good food, that the climate was perfect, and what superb equipment they had.
PARALLEL PARTICIPLES	The old house was *battered* by the rain and *bleached* by the sun.
NOT PARALLEL	The old house was battered by the rain and there was no color left because it was standing in the open sunlight.

If possible, balance parallel ideas by expressing them in approximately the same number of words, the same kind of words, and in identical or closely similar word order.

NEITHER PARALLEL NOR BALANCED	He was a good merchant, but was very poor at keeping books.
PARALLEL AND BALANCED	He was a *good merchant,* but a *poor bookkeeper.*
NEITHER PARALLEL NOR BALANCED	He believed in democracy for the upper classes, but felt that the common people should be ruled by their superiors.
PARALLEL AND BALANCED	He believed in *democracy for the classes,* but *autocracy for the masses.*
PARALLEL AND BALANCED	It is wiser *to invest than to squander, to seek out friends than to collect acquaintances, to treasure life than to throw it away.*

Notice how parallelism, balance, and repetition are combined in the following celebrated passage from I Corinthians 13:

Though I speak with the tongues of men and of angels, and have not charity, I am become as sounding brass, or a tinkling cymbal. And though I have the gift of prophecy, and understand all mysteries, and all knowledge; and though I have all faith, so that I could remove mountains, and have not charity, I am nothing. And though I bestow all my goods to feed the poor, and though I give my body to be burned, and have not charity, it profiteth me nothing.

Charity suffereth long, and is kind; charity envieth not; charity vaunteth not itself, is not puffed up, doth not behave herself unseemly, seeketh not her own, is not easily provoked, thinketh no evil; rejoiceth not in iniquity, but rejoiceth in the truth; beareth all things, believeth all things, hopeth all things, endureth all things.

Charity never faileth: but whether there be prophecies, they shall fail; whether there be tongues, they shall cease; whether there be knowledge, it shall vanish away. For we know in part, and we prophesy in part. But when that which is perfect is come, then that which is in part shall be done away.

When I was a child, I spake as a child, I understood as a child, I thought as a child: but when I became a man, I put away childish things. For now we see through a glass darkly; but then face to face; now I know in part; but then shall I know even as also I am known. And now abideth faith, hope, charity, these three; but the greatest of these is charity.

23 CONSISTENCY

In dealing with any subject, decide in advance on the method of treating the subject. Then endeavor to be consistent, avoiding such departures from the selected method as might creep in through carelessness or forgetfulness.

23 A CONSISTENCY IN TENSE

When writing a narrative, decide on a basic tense and do not change it unless the reference to some prior or subsequent event demands a change.

INCONSISTENT   John *sprang* to his feet when he *heard* the whistle. He *ran* as fast as he could to reach the upper deck. There he *sees* a battleship bearing down on them. [Inconsistent change to present tense] He *would remember* that moment for years to come. [Consistent because the reference is to the future]

23 B CONSISTENCY IN NUMBER

When discussing a type or a class, decide in advance whether to use the singular or plural number and do not change it.

INCONSISTENT   The automatic washing *machine* is a great
                invention. *It* saves *housewives* many hours
                of drudgery. *These machines* are among
                the most wonderful inventions of the
                twentieth century.

CONSISTENT   The automatic washing *machine* is a great
                invention. It saves the *housewife* many
                hours of drudgery. This *machine* is *one*
                of the most wonderful inventions of the
                twentieth century.

23 C CONSISTENCY IN PERSON

Decide in advance whether a piece of writing is to be personal
or impersonal, and do not change the point of view.

INCONSISTENT   When learning to play a piano, *the student*
                should remember that great care and pre-
                cision are essential. *You* should practice
                simple pieces until they are completely
                mastered. *One* can never succeed in an art
                if the fundamentals are neglected.

In this paragraph, either the *You* in the second sentence should
be changed to *He* or the entire paragraph should be written as
a direct appeal to the reader, as:

   When learning to play a piano, remember that great care
   and precision are essential. You should practice simple pieces
   until they are completely mastered. You can never succeed in
   an art if you neglect the fundamentals.

23 D CONSISTENCY AND APPROPRIATENESS IN TONE

Unless you wish to jar the reader by some sudden intrusion,
keep the tone and level of writing constant. Informal or chatty
writing admits the use of slang or colloquialisms which are out

of keeping with formal writing. The appropriateness of words in given contexts is learned only by reading and listening. But notice the absurdity of the following:

The dean exhorted the statutory members of the faculty to redouble their efforts and *get going*.

I get sick and tired of hearing you squawk about your *lassitude*.

Fourscore and seven years ago, our fathers brought forth on this continent a new nation, conceived in Liberty, and dedicated to the proposition that *highbrows are no better than lowbrows*.

There are many synonyms in the English language which, although nearly identical in meaning, are appropriately used only in certain connections. The word *love* means *zero*, but only in the game of tennis. *Tip, gratuity,* and *perquisite* all mean some kind of value received as incidental and variable rather than as fixed income. In normal usage, however, the word *tip* is connected with frequent small amounts of money for trivial services, *gratuity* with a considerable sum of money in reward for lengthy service, and the word *perquisite* applies to certain emoluments or values which accompany political offices and some professions. Similarly, *salary, pay, wage, fee,* and *honorarium* are roughly synonymous, but are applicable to different types and levels of monetary remuneration. When taking a position, a lawyer is *retained*, a laborer is *hired*, a minister is *called*, a clerk is *employed*, a physician is *consulted*.

Be observant of word usage in your reading. When consulting a dictionary, read the entire entry, not just one of the definitions, to get as much of a sense of the word as possible.

24 VARIETY

The type of sentence structure appropriate to a given piece of writing depends on the nature of the subject, the purpose of the author, and the anticipated audience. Directions, for example, should be written in simple language and short sentences.

To reach the Denby Road Church:

1. Follow Route 4 to Carmine Street.
2. Turn right and continue to the second traffic signal (Denby Road).
3. Turn left on Denby Road.
4. You will see the church on the right hand side of the street.

Short, direct sentences are also effective in describing action:

A succession of loud and shrill screams, bursting suddenly from the throat of the chained form, seemed to thrust me violently back. For a brief moment I hesitated—I trembled. Unsheathing my rapier, I began to grope with it about the recess; but the thought of an instant reassured me. I placed my hand upon the solid fabric of the catacombs, and felt satisfied. I reapproached the wall. I replied to the yells of him who clamored. I re-echoed—I aided—I surpassed them in volume and in strength. I did this, and the clamorer grew still.

—Edgar Allan Poe, "The Cask of Amontillado"

In other kinds of writing where no special effect is sought for, avoid monotony by varying the lengths of sentences and by avoiding a series of sentences with nearly identical structure and word order, such as occur in the following example:

When I was a boy, my comrades and I had only one permanent ambition: to be steamboatmen. Although we had transient ambitions of other sorts, they were only transient. When a circus came and went, it left us all burning to become clowns. When the first negro minstrel show came to town, we all wanted to try that kind of life. Every once in a while, we all had the ambition to become pirates. Although all of these ambitions gradually faded out, the ambition to be steamboatmen always remained.

Essentially the same material is given variety and interest by sentences of varied length and structure in Mark Twain's *Life on the Mississippi:*

When I was a boy, there was but one permanent ambition among my comrades in our village on the west bank of the Mississippi River. That was, to be a steamboatman. We had transient ambitions of other sorts, but they were only transient. When a circus came and went, it left us all burning to become clowns; the first negro minstrel show that ever came to our section left us all suffering to try that kind of life; now and then we had a hope that, if we lived and were good, God would permit us to be pirates. These ambitions faded out, each in its turn; but the ambition to be a steamboatman always remained.

In the following selection, the opening of William Hazlitt's essay *On Familiar Style,* notice how the first short, direct sentence attracts attention. Then notice the varied length of the second, third, and fourth sentences which are followed by an effective parallelism in the fifth sentence. The sixth sentence, quite long, acts as a kind of summation.

[1.] It is not easy to write a familiar style. [2.] Many people mistake a familiar for a vulgar style, and suppose that to write without affectation is to write at random. [3.] On the contrary, there is nothing that requires more precision, and, if I may say so, purity of expression, than the style I am speaking of. [4.] It utterly rejects not only all unmeaning pomp, but all low, cant phrases, and loose, unconnected, *slipshod* allusions. [5.] It is not to take the first word that offers, but the best word in common use; it is not to throw words together in any combinations we please, but to follow and avail ourselves of the true idiom of the language. [6.] To write a genuine familiar or truly English style, is to write as any one would speak in common conversation, who had a thorough command and choice of words, or who could discourse with ease, force, and perspicuity, setting aside all pedantic and oratorical flourishes.

· PUNCTUATION

Punctuation is a device used to assist the reader. It takes the place of changes in tone, inflection, and volume, and of pauses, facial expressions, etc. by which a speaker makes his meaning clear.

25 TERMINAL PUNCTUATION

25 A THE PERIOD

The principal use of the period is to indicate the end of a sentence which is not a question or an exclamation.

The president was elected.   [statement]

I asked if he would see me.   [indirect question]

Please shut the door.   [request or command]

The period is often used for terminal purposes when a sentence is not involved, as after numbers in a list:

1. The President
2. The Council
3. The Board of Trustees

The period is used to terminate most abbreviations:

e.g., i. e., Mr., Dr., Rev., etc.

Three periods are used to indicate the omission of one or more words or even sentences in a quotation:

"I pledge allegiance . . . to the republic . . ."

When the omission occurs after the end of a sentence, the three periods are added after the period which terminates the sentence:

"Shakespeare was born in 1564. . . . He married Anne Hathaway in 1582."

25 B   THE QUESTION MARK

The question mark is used to terminate a direct question of any sort:

Who are you? Why? Why not? He did?

When enclosed in parentheses, the question mark indicates uncertainty or doubt:

He lived from 1635 (?) to 1680.

25 C   THE EXCLAMATION MARK

Use the exclamation mark to terminate a strong expression of feeling. Do not use it for indications of mild emotion.

Nonsense! I don't believe you.

I'll shoot the first man who moves!

Get out of this house at once!

Be sparing in the use of exclamations. The effectiveness of exclamation marks is dulled by over use.

26 THE COMMA

The comma is the most frequently used (and abused) aid to reading. Most poor users of commas annoy their readers by inserting illogical commas or too many commas. There is no need for uncertainty if the basic principles governing the use of the comma are clearly understood.

26 A TO SEPARATE PARTS OF A SERIES

(1) Use the comma to separate words, phrases, or clauses in a series. It is a substitute for a coordinating conjunction.

John, Fred, Harry, Frank

[John and Fred and Harry and Frank]

Usually the final element in the series is preceded by *and* or *or* to indicate the nature and the termination of the series.

John, Fred, Harry, and Frank

A comma before the terminating conjunction (*and* or *or*), although not absolutely essential, is used to prevent confusion because of the not infrequent appearance of *and* within the members of a series:

She shopped at Johnson's, Ward and Nelson's, and French's.

He ate soup, meat and potatoes, and pie.

He went across the sidewalk, down the street, and into the bar and grill.

She asked to see the manager, she complained about the merchandise and the service, and she got satisfaction.

(2) TO SET OFF ADJECTIVES IN A SERIES

A single adjective modifying a noun is frequently so necessary that it may be considered a part of the identification: *pine* tree, *drinking* glass, *red* dress. Another adjective preceding such an adjective-noun phrase functions as if it modified the entire phrase and is therefore not separated from the phrase by a comma: *tall* pine tree, *large* drinking glass, *beautiful* red dress.

To call attention to each adjective as individually and separately describing the noun, use a comma to separate the adjectives:

> a tall, dark, distinguished gentleman

A comma between adjectives has the same effect as the conjunction *and*.

> a tall and dark and distinguished gentleman

26 B TO SEPARATE THE CLAUSES OF A COMPOUND SENTENCE JOINED BY A COORDINATING CONJUNCTION

Use the comma to separate the independent clauses of a compound sentence when they are joined by a coordinating conjunction. The comma is placed immediately before the conjunction (*and, but, or, nor, for, yet*) to indicate that the conjunction introduces a clause.

> The mayor invited the members of the committee to lunch, and most of them accepted his invitation.

> I haven't succeeded in balancing my checkbook, yet I plan to continue writing checks.

When the clauses are very short so that most or all of the sentence can be taken in instantaneously by the eye, the comma is not required.

> He sent for her and she came.

26 C
TO SEPARATE INTERJECTIONS AND SIMILAR NON-INTEGRATED SENTENCE ELEMENTS

Occasionally, words or phrases in a sentence are not integrated in the sentence structure. That is, they do not modify specific words, they are not subjects or verbs, they are not objects of prepositions, etc. Separate such non-integrated words or phrases from the remainder of the sentence by commas.

(1) Use the comma to set off interjections which are included in sentences.

> *Oh*, I thought so.

> *Hey*, watch your step!

> *Hello*, I'm glad to see you.

If the interjection occurs within the sentence, it is separated by two commas.

> I tried so hard, *alas*, to do it.

Use the comma to set off any other words or phrases which behave as interjections:
The adverbs *yes, no* are frequently used as interjections.

> *Yes*, I'll be glad to.

Terms of direct address are normally used as interjections.

> *John*, get the book.

> *You over there*, put on your hat.

(2) Use the comma to set off sentence modifiers. Words like *however, moreover, furthermore, therefore, nevertheless* and phrases like *on the other hand, in addition, to the contrary* often modify the whole sentence instead of a single word within the sentence. To make clear that they are not intended to modify a single word, separate them from the rest of the sentence by commas.

However, she caught the train.

He tried, *moreover,* to attain his goal.

On the other hand, he wasted his money.

(3) Use the comma to set off absolute phrases. An absolute phrase, made up of a noun or pronoun and a participle (*the sun having risen*), is another kind of sentence modifier. Absolute phrases are not connected to the remainder of the sentence by relating words such as prepositions or conjunctions. They are therefore set off by commas.

The river being cold, we did not go swimming.

It seemed sensible, *the weather being warm,* to pack a lunch.

26 D TO SET OFF A LONG PHRASE OR CLAUSE PRECEDING THE SUBJECT

Since the first element in an English sentence is normally its subject, any phrase or clause of five words or more preceding the subject is concluded with a comma to indicate that the subject is about to appear.

During the long winter of 1881, the king suffered a severe illness.

When I see robins on the lawn, I know that spring is here.

Having reached the age of discretion, she was no longer supervised.

If the phrase is so short that the reader can take in both the phrase and the subject in a single eye-fixation, the comma is not necessary.

In 1881 the king suffered a severe illness.

26 E TO INDICATE INTERRUPTIONS OF NORMAL WORD ORDER

Set off by commas: words, phrases, or clauses which interrupt normal word order. Normally, adjectives precede the nouns they modify, and, normally, subjects are followed by verbs or by modifying phrases or clauses:

The old and respected firm in the city went bankrupt.

If, for purpose of emphasis, the adjectives *old* and *respected* follow the noun *firm*, they are set off by commas:

The firm, old and respected, went bankrupt.

A single comma should never interrupt the natural flow of a sentence, as from subject to verb or from verb to complement. But intruding elements of any kind should be indicated by being preceded and followed by commas.

The river, it seems likely, will overflow its banks.

The year of his graduation, 1950, was an eventful one.

She was a tall and, to put it mildly, buxom woman.

26 F TO SET OFF NONRESTRICTIVE ELEMENTS

Any word, phrase, or clause that is not essential to the meaning of a sentence is called nonrestrictive. Set off nonrestrictive elements by commas.

Some words, like *scurrilous*, are difficult to spell.

His father, Mr. Smith, was ill.

The Homeric epics, the *Iliad* and the *Odyssey*, are long poems.

His uncle, who is a doctor, is coming for a visit.

Be careful to distinguish between such nonrestrictive elements and restrictive elements. Restrictive words, phrases, or clauses are necessary to the meaning of the sentence and are never set off by commas.

Shakespeare's play *Hamlet* is a masterpiece.

[The name of the play is essential to the meaning.]

Dante's epic, *The Divine Comedy,* is made up of one hundred cantos.

[It is Dante's only epic; its name is therefore not essential.]

The people who sat in the balcony paid less for their seats.

[The clause *who sat in the balcony* is restrictive.]

My brother, who sat in the balcony, enjoyed the play.

[The location of his seat is not considered essential to the statement being made.]

By insertion or omission of commas, the writer can indicate whether elements are restrictive or not.

His dog Rover is a collie.

[The lack of commas indicates that he has several dogs. One of them is named Rover.]

His dog, Rover, is a collie.

[He owns only one dog. The name is given but it is not essential.]

When the nonrestrictive elements occurs at the end of the sentence, the comma preceding it indicates its relative unimportance.

The president was interviewed by a large group of reporters, who were informally dressed.

26 G TO SEPARATE CONTRASTED SENTENCE ELEMENTS

Use the comma to emphasize the contrast between two parts of a sentence.

He wanted to see a psychiatrist, not a lawyer.

His diet was wholesome, not appetizing.

She longed to find happiness, but found misery instead.

26 H TO PREVENT MISREADING

Use the comma to prevent misreading when the sequence of words in a sentence might lead to momentary confusion.

During the summer, days become longer.

Without the comma, the reader might well read *summer days* as adjective-noun.

Father sent the car for John, didn't he?

Without the comma, the reader might read *for* as a conjunction and *John* as the subject of the verb *did*.

The lawyer interviewed John and Fred, and seemed very happy about what they had to say.

In this sentence the two *and's* occur in close proximity. The first joins the nouns *John* and *Fred;* the second joins the verbs *interviewed* and *seemed*. The comma after *Fred* clarifies the structure of the sentence.

26 I CONVENTIONAL USES OF THE COMMA

Certain uses of the comma (where other punctuation marks might do as well) have become established by convention.

Following the salutation of an informal letter: *Dear Mildred,*

Following the complimentary close of a letter: *Yours truly,*

Separating dates of the month from the year: *June 19, 1942*

Separating parts of an address: *Mr. John Smith, 138 Elm Street, Syracuse 3, N. Y.*

Separating numbered or lettered divisions or subdivisions: *Book III, Chapter 9;* or *III, 9;* or *A, d*

Separating names from distinguishing titles: *Frank Jones, Jr.* or *Edward French, Ph.D.*

Separating thousands in large figures: *1,497,341*

Separating a direct quotation from the indication of the speaker (See Sec. 34.)

Placed before and after introductory words and abbreviations such as *i. e., e.g., for example:*

Some plays are known as closet dramas, i. e., they were written to be read rather than acted.

27 MISUSE OF THE COMMA

Do not annoy the reader by inserting commas where they are not required. Commas are intended to help the reader; unnecessary commas only confuse him.

27 A Do not interrupt the normal flow of thought by a comma.

WRONG The fact that the train had broken down halfway between its point of departure and its destination, was sufficient reason for the passengers to malign the railroad.

[The subject is a long clause, but it is entirely clear. It opens the sentence as expected, and it is followed immediately by the verb. Inserting a comma after *destination* merely impedes the flow of thought.]

WRONG   The carpenter insisted, that he knew what he was doing.

[The comma after *insisted* separates the verb from its object.]

WRONG   He drove a hard, sharp, painful, bargain.

[The comma after *painful* separates the adjective *painful* from the word it modifies.]

27 B   **Do not separate words or phrases joined by *and* or *or*.**

WRONG   He went to the office, and opened his mail.

[*And* joins the compound verb *went* and *opened*. It does not join two clauses.]

27 C   **Do not place a comma between a conjunction and the word or words it introduces.**

WRONG   He was tired but, he refused to stop driving.

WRONG   The lonely woman continued to hope that, her son was still alive.

28   THE SEMICOLON

The semicolon functions midway between the comma and the period as an indication of a pause. It is stronger than the comma and weaker than the period.

28 A   TO SEPARATE INDEPENDENT CLAUSES

The principal use of the semicolon is to mark the dividing point in a compound sentence, the clauses of which are not joined by a coordinating conjunction.

The policeman stood on the corner; he was watching the traffic pattern at the intersection.

The boss had a good sense of humor; nevertheless, he was a strict supervisor.

28 B   TO SEPARATE MAJOR WORD GROUPINGS FROM LESSER ONES

A proliferation of commas in a sentence may lead to confusion. The semicolon, as a stronger mark, is therefore useful in punctuating major elements which themselves contain commas.

He visited several colleges, schools, and institutions; several factories, office-buildings, and churches; and a number of public buildings of a miscellaneous nature.

[The three major divisions, the first two of which contain commas, are clarified by the use of the semicolon.]

The old horse, tired and hungry after its long journey over the long, hilly, rutted country roads, finally staggered and fell; and it was a long time before it could be persuaded to get up again.

[The individual clauses of the compound sentence, the first of which contains several commas, are clearly indicated by the semicolon.]

29   THE COLON

The colon means *as follows*. It is principally used to introduce a list (frequently in conjunction with such words as *following* or *as follows*). It should not be used to introduce a short list such as *He raised beans, peas, apples, pears, and plums.*

The gentlemen who contributed to the fund were: John Doe, Frank Smith, Eliot Doolittle, Ezra Jones, Samuel

Greenbaum, John MacMillan, Edward Stritch, James Hoffman, Nelson Brown.

The principles on which the club was founded are as follows:

1. The establishment of a revolving fund for education.
2. The provision of entertainment for the children.
3. Monthly social meetings for the adults.

Occasionally the colon is used to introduce a single word or phrase to add dramatic significance.

He had only one thing to live for: death.

The colon can be used to introduce a single word, phrase, or clause when it acts as a substitute for the words *as a result*.

The president died: the firm failed.

The colon is used after the salutation of a business letter (*Dear Sir:* or *To Whom It May Concern:*) and to divide subdivisions from major divisions as in recording time (*12:25*) or Biblical references (*Genesis 10:3*).

30 THE DASH

The dash is used to indicate a sharp or sudden break in the normal or expected flow of sentence structure. (In typing, a dash is represented by two hyphens.)

He asked me—what was he thinking?—to marry him.

I hoped that he—. But I'd rather not talk about it.

The dash may be used to separate parenthetical ideas or ideas inserted as an afterthought.

PARENTHETICAL　　The New York skyline—especially when viewed for the first time—is a breathtaking sight.

AFTERTHOUGHT　　He ran down the hill with the speed of an express train—or so it seemed.

The dash is used in dialogue to describe hesitating or halting speech.

"I mean—I think—I think I mean," he began hesitantly. "I think I mean I'd make a good husband."

31　THE HYPHEN

The hyphen is used to make a compound word out of two or more words which are intended to be read as a single unit.

The Dartmouth-Brown game

Mr. John King-Smith

A high-pressure salesman

A sugar-coated pill

A holier-than-thou expression

The man-with-a-smile makes friends.

The hyphen is used to eliminate ambiguities or misreadings which occasionally result from the addition of a prefix.

re-educate　re-align　re-cover

The hyphen is used to indicate that the remainder of a word is to follow when the word is broken at the end of a line. Words may not be divided arbitrarily; they may be broken only between syllables. (Syllables are the parts of a word which are naturally pronounced as units. When in doubt about correct division into syllables, consult a good dictionary.)

> Samuel Johnson, who was an outstanding literary figure of the eighteenth century in England, was known as the great lexicographer. He compiled the first real English dictionary.

The hyphen is used with compound numbers from twenty-one to ninety-nine.

The hyphen is used to separate dates of births and death: *John Barton (1181-1214)*, scores of games: *13-12*, and other figures where the relationship between them is obvious.

32 THE APOSTROPHE

Apart from indicating possession (See Sec. 1 C), the apostrophe is principally used to indicate missing letters in a contraction.

> Who's there? I can't come.

The apostrophe is also used to form plurals of letters, figures, or signs for which there is no acceptable plural.

> There are three 9's, twenty-seven n's, and two *'s on the page.

33 PARENTHESES AND BRACKETS

Parentheses are used to enclose materials which are so intrusive as to be an annoying interruption of sentence structure.

> It is important (importance being understood to be a relative matter) to obey the law.

> The law was passed (1) to satisfy the governor, (2) to please the people, and (3) to provide greater safety.

> The houses were classified as (a) bungalows, (b) ranch-type houses, (c) split-level houses.

> His novel *The Homeward Trail* (1917) was a best-seller.

Brackets are used to enclose additions by the editor to any kind of quoted matter.

"The author [Mark Twain] was known primarily as a humorist."

"He was born in 1835 [?] in a small southern town."

34 QUOTATIONS AND QUOTATION MARKS

34 A QUOTATION MARKS TO INDICATE TITLES

Quotation marks are used to indicate titles of short works such as articles in magazines, short stories, one-act plays, one-reel motion pictures, essays, short poems, chapter titles, etc.

"The Raven" [short poem]

"The Murders in the Rue Morgue" [short story]

"Bound East for Cardiff" [one-act play]

34 B DIRECT QUOTATIONS

Quoted materials, whether oral or written, are indicated by being enclosed in quotation marks. Only the exact words of the original speaker or writer should be so enclosed. An indirect quotation or a report of the substance of what was said or written should not be enclosed by quotation marks.

DIRECT   He said, "I am going home."

INDIRECT   He said that he was going home.

DIRECT   She said, "I have a headache. I am going to bed."

INDIRECT   She said that her head hurt and that she was going to bed.

DIRECT   The opening words of the chapter are "I continued at home with my wife and children."

INDIRECT   The opening words of the chapter state that the author stayed at home with his wife and children.

COMBINED   She said that she had "no intentions" of staying.

In direct quotations, indications of the speaker (*he said, she asked*) are separated from the quotation by a comma or marked off by two commas if reference to the speaker is placed within a sentence.

"Please don't tell my mother," he whined.

The nurse replied, "That's exactly what I intend to do."

"Well, at least," he entreated, "don't tell her everything."

When the indication of the speaker is placed at the end of a quotation which concludes with a question mark or an exclamation mark, the comma is omitted.

"Don't you know enough to stop?" he asked.

"Let me go!" she shrieked.

If the quotation consists of more than one sentence, only one sentence is joined to the indication of the speaker.

"My son wants to buy this," she said. "How much will it cost?"

"I wouldn't do that," he remonstrated. "You might get into trouble."

In quotations other than dialogue, the punctuation and capitalization of quoted matter is reproduced exactly as it was originally written.

The author believes that "Capitalism is here to stay."

The novel reflected the author's "growing concern with the problem of juvenile delinquency."

If the quotation is longer than one paragraph, no end-quotation marks are placed at the conclusion of the first paragraph. All succeeding paragraphs are prefaced by quotation marks, but only the final paragraph is concluded with end-quotation marks.

Long quotations (ten lines or more) from writings are not enclosed in quotation marks. They are set off from the original writing by indentation. Smaller typeface is customary for printed matter and single spacing for typewritten material.

34 C QUOTATIONS WITHIN QUOTATIONS

Single quotation marks are used to indicate a quotation within a quotation.

"I've just read Shelley's 'Ode to the West Wind,' " she said.

The alternation of double and single quotation marks is continued for the inclusion of quotations within quotations within other quotations. Such complexities should be avoided, of course, but the following is an example of the technique:

"Are you aware," asked the lawyer, "that the defendant precisely stated, 'I did not read "The Bride Said, 'No' " ' ?"

Be sure that all opening quotation marks are balanced by end-quotation marks.

34 D QUOTATION MARKS USED WITH OTHER PUNCTUATION

The placing of quotation marks in connection with other punctuation follows the standard procedures instituted by printers for the sake of the physical appearance of the page. Periods and commas are always placed inside end-quotation marks.

"I wanted," he said, "to go home."

Colons and semicolons are always placed outside end-quotation marks. Other marks are placed where they logically belong— within the quotation if they punctuate the quotation, outside the quotation if they punctuate the sentence of which the quotation is a part.

He called his friend "old frog"; he didn't mean it as an insult.

He assimilated the advice given in the pamphlet "How to Study": he passed the course.

"How are you?" I asked.

How can I tell that "Whatever is, is right"?

Beware of "the valley of the shadow of death"!

34 E PUNCTUATION OF DIALOGUE

Standard practice in the punctuation of dialogue calls for a new paragraph for each change of speaker. Descriptive or other materials related to the speaker are contained in the same paragraph as the quotation.

"I knew it!" said the toper to the shepherd with much satisfaction. "When I walked up your garden before coming in, and saw the hives all of a row, I said to myself, 'Where there's bees, there's honey, and where there's honey, there's mead.' But mead of such a truly comfortable sort as this I really didn't expect to meet in my older days." He took yet another pull at the mug, till it assumed an ominous elevation.

"Glad you enjoy it!" said the shepherd, warmly.

"It is a goodish mead," assented Mrs. Fennel, with an absence of enthusiasm which seemed to say that it was possible to buy praise for one's cellar at too heavy a price. "It is trouble enough to make, and really I hardly think we shall make any more. For honey sells well, and we ourselves can make shift with a drop o' small mead and metheglin for common use from the comb-washings."

"Oh, but you'll never have the heart!" reproachfully cried the stranger in cinder-gray, after taking up the mug a third time and setting it down empty.

"I love mead when 'tis old like this, as I love to go to church o' Sundays, or to relieve the needy any day of the week."

"Ha, ha, ha!" said the man in the chimney-corner, who, in spite of the taciturnity induced by the pipe of tobacco, could not or would not refrain from this slight testimony to his comrade's humor.

—Thomas Hardy, "The Three Strangers"

A particular advantage of this convention is that when only two speakers are involved, the alternation of paragraphs makes it unnecessary to identify each speaker in turn and allows the dialogue to be paced more rapidly and without interruptions.

"Everybody believed the story, didn't they?" said the dirty-faced man, refilling his pipe.

"Except Tom's enemies," replied the bagman. "Some of 'em said Tom invented it altogether; and others said he was drunk, and fancied it, and got hold of the wrong trousers by mistake before he went to bed. But nobody ever minded what *they* said."

"Tom said it was all true?"

"Every word."

"And your uncle?"

"Every letter."

"They must have been very nice men, both of 'em," said the dirty-faced man.

"Yes, they were," replied the bagman; "very nice men indeed!"

—Charles Dickens, "The Bagman's Story"

35 ITALICS

Italics is a term used to designate a particular font of printer's type in which the letters slant upwards to the right as in the word *italics*. In written or typed material, italics are indicated by underlining.

35 A ITALICS TO INDICATE TITLES OF FULL-LENGTH WORKS

Use italics to indicate the titles of novels, full-length plays, long book-length poems, full-length motion pictures, and the titles of books in general. They are also used to indicate names of magazines or periodical publications of any sort. This usage in conjunction with quotation marks helps to distinguish the chapter from the complete book, the poem from the collection in which it appears, the article from the magazine, etc.

   Hamlet   A Tale of Two Cities   The Atlantic Monthly

EXCEPTIONS: Through convention, the Bible and the books of the Bible are neither italicized nor put in quotation marks. The place of publication of newspapers (normally regarded as part of the title) is frequently neither italicized nor put in quotation marks.

   Genesis   The New York *Times*   The Iowa *Gazette*

35 B ITALICS TO INDICATE WORDS OR LETTERS USED AS SUCH

Use italics to indicate words or letters which are used as such, that is, words or letters considered independent of their meaning.

   The word *benign* is sometimes misspelled.

   The letter *I* should be capitalized when used alone.

35 C ITALICS FOR EMPHASIS

Italics are occasionally used (though very rarely) to give emphasis to a particular word or group of words. This usage should be avoided and resorted to only when no other method of stressing the word is available, as in the reporting of dialogue or in the writing of plays.

   "I didn't mean your husband; I meant *you!*"

·THE PARAGRAPH

Paragraphs are the structural units of composition. An essay or a narrative consists of a group of related paragraphs that develop the thought of the whole. To write logically and effectively, therefore, one must master the principles of paragraphing.

36 THE PARAGRAPH DEFINED

Thoughts are stated in sentences, but they are developed in paragraphs. Whereas a sentence states that May is a lovely month, a paragraph develops the statement by expressing the qualities of sunshine and warmth, of gentle rains, and of blossoming that make May a lovely month. A paragraph, therefore, is a group of related sentences that expand a statement by explaining it, or illustrating it, or proving it. A paragraph gives a statement substance and weight, invests it with meaning, and charges it with conviction. A reader may miss or dismiss a statement, but he is held by a paragraph and urged to understand and believe.

Just as a paragraph contains a group of related sentences, an essay or narrative contains a group of related paragraphs. Each paragraph develops a logical unit of thought. Each paragraph is logically related to the paragraph that precedes it and to the paragraph that follows. All of the paragraphs combine to express the design and purpose of the whole. Therefore, paragraphs are, as already stated, the structural units of composition.

A paragraph is also a device of punctuation. The indented first line identifies the paragraph, separates it from the preceding and following paragraphs, and shows where a thought begins and ends. Physically the paragraph breaks what would otherwise be a solid block of writing into small units, thus giving the reader some relief. The reader may pause between paragraphs, mark his progress, and read on with a sense of direction.

Although paragraphs usually contain several sentences, undeveloped paragraphs of one or two sentences are frequently used for the following purposes:

1. In essays, to summarize what has been said, to guide the reader from section to section, or to emphasize an important point.
2. In dialogue, to indicate a new speech or a new speaker. A paragraph of dialogue may therefore contain only a phrase or a word:

> "Are you Frank Jones?" he asked.
> "Yes."
> "And you live here?"
> "I do."

3. In newspapers, to make the layout attractive and to express facts and opinions simply and emphatically.

Normally, however, a paragraph states a topic, develops it, relates it to other paragraphs, and contributes to the design and purpose of the whole essay. In short, a paragraph is, as already stated, a logical unit of composition. Any one who wishes to write clearly and logically must be able to plan and write paragraphs.

36 A   Indent the first line of every paragraph an inch in handwritten manuscripts and five spaces in typescript.

The next morning we arose before dawn. Mother made breakfast, and father loaded the car. . . .

36 B Develop the paragraph with material suitable to the topic.

The kinds of substance and the methods most commonly used to develop paragraphs are the following:

1. PARTICULARS AND DETAILS

The Shelburne Museum is a delightful place to visit. It is an outdoor museum in a shallow bowl of meadowland with the Green Mountains rising in the distance. The entrance to the Museum is a covered bridge across a little brook and through a thicket of vines and bushes to a parking lot, discreetly hidden by a grove of trees. It is a museum in the fields broken by little dips and rises and by groves of trees with picnic tables and fireplaces for the visitors. A narrow road runs around the field like a belt, and on it runs an open truck with a low platform and a row of benches on either side, proceeding so slowly that passengers can hop off and on with ease, or they can wait for it to stop at one of the designated stations. Scattered in the fields, none very far from the road and the little truck, are the exhibits: an inn, several houses with their original furnishings, and a prison with stocks—all from the Colonial period; a general store, of course; a one-room school house from grandfather's day; another store crowded with antique clocks and music boxes and mechanical toys; a nineteenth-century steam locomotive, and best of all, perhaps, the last ferry boat to ply Lake Champlain. It is a strange sensation to see the old side-wheeler landlocked on the side of a small hill, and stranger still to stand on its deck and look out over acres of greenery. One feels, perhaps, a little like Noah when the ark came to rest, at last, on Mount Ararat.

[In this paragraph, details about the appearance of the Museum and its exhibits are presented to develop the initial statement that the Shelburne Museum is a delightful place to visit.]

2. INSTANCES AND EXAMPLES

His life has been a series of brilliant ideas, early successes, and ultimate failures. His experience with diaper service is typical. He was the first to think of a laundry that would supply mothers with diapers and wash them for a reasonable fee. He worked out all of the details, including the container to hold the soiled diapers. He secured financial backing, organized a company, and directed its initial operations. But as the service took hold and the company began to make large profits, he lost interest. The activity was no longer novel; the necessary supervision, the close attention to detail, became onerous. His mind was already occupied with another idea and another promotional campaign. Inevitably the customers dwindled, and so did the profits before the onslaught of other companies offering better service. His backers warned and complained and finally removed him from control. He left without regret and with only a little money that he was ready to invest in another idea, more brilliant than the last, that would make him a millionaire.

[Here the initial statement about the pattern of his life is illustrated by the example of the diaper service.]

3. LOGICAL DIVISIONS—REASONS, CLASSES, STEPS IN A PROCESS

It [*The Impressions and Reflections of a Superannuated Man* by Sir Francis Denby-Johns] is, rather, three books in one. The first is a romantic and fascinating account of the young explorer (fresh impressions and impromptu judgments from the entries in his diary during the early years). The next presents the reminiscent Denby-Johns (reflective commentaries, "fillers," explanations and revisions of the original entries.) The third book may be said to consist of Langsam's narrative and interpretive connectives. *The Impressions and Reflections of a Superannuated Man* contains fewer entries from the diaries than did *Fair Horizons* and is consequently less interesting than that volume to the general reader and more interesting to students of archeology and ethnology.

[In this paragraph the book being reviewed is shown to consist of three parts or kinds of material.]

4. COMPARISON AND CONTRAST

The harpsichord is the most important forerunner of the piano. The harpsichord is somewhat smaller and more delicate than a grand piano, but looks like a grand piano except that it is tail-shaped rather than rounded or curved. Whereas the piano has only one keyboard, the harpsichord has two. Like the piano, the harpsichord has several strings to a key, but the strings of the harpsichord are vibrated by the plucking action of jacks rather than by the striking of hammers, as in the piano. The strings of the piano are controlled by dampers and pedals, but in a harpsichord the strings are controlled by stops, similar to those of an organ. Compared to the piano, the harpsichord is rather weak in tone and tinny; it cannot jump abruptly around the keyboard, and it is not capable of strong accents. On the other hand, the harpsichord can make more sounds to a key and is capable of such a variety of sounds that it frequently seems to be two different instruments. The harpsichord is different from a piano, but not inferior to it. For the music of its day, the music composed for it, the harpsichord is unequalled.

[In this paragraph the harpsichord is explained by means of comparison with the more familiar piano. The explanation proceeds by showing how the harpsichord is similar to the piano and different from it.]

5. ANALOGY

Poetry produces an illusion on the eye of the mind, as a magic lantern produces an illusion on the eye of the body. And, as the magic lantern acts best in a dark room, poetry effects its purpose most completely in a dark age. As the light of knowledge breaks upon its exhibition, as the outlines of certainty become more and more definite, and the shades of probability more and more distinct, the hues and lineaments of the phantoms which the poet calls up grow fainter and fainter. We cannot unite the incompatible advantages of reality and deception, the clear discernment of truth and the exquisite enjoyment of fiction.

[In this essay on Milton, Thomas Babington Macaulay uses the analogy of the magic lantern to explain the illusion produced by poetry. Macaulay also compares the figurative "eye of the mind" with the "eye of the body."]

6. DEFINITION

In the folowing paragraph the term *communist* is defined by the beliefs he holds and by his formal political affiliation.

A communist is one who accepts the economic principles and theories of Marx, Engels, Lenin, and possibly Stalin. He believes that the means of production should be owned by the workers. He accepts the slogan: from each according to his ability, to each according to his needs. He would establish socialism through the dictatorship of the proletariat in a state which would gradually wither away as the ideal socialist society evolves. He believes that the evolution of the socialist state will come about from the education of the masses and as a result of historical conditions, including the nature of capitalism and its destructive contradictions. He believes, also, that in their progress toward socialism the proletariat may be compelled, by the forces of reaction, to resort to force and violence. In addition to accepting these ideas and principles, the communist may also, of course, be a member of one of the communist parties of the world.

7. CAUSE AND EFFECT

In *The Life of Addison* Thomas Babington Macaulay ascribes certain faults in Addison's character to the adulation of a coterie of inferiors with whom he surrounded himself.

To the excessive modesty of Addison's nature, we must ascribe another fault which generally arises from a very different cause. He became a little too fond of seeing himself surrounded by a small circle of admirers, to whom he was as a King or rather as a God. All of these men were inferior to him in ability, and some of them had very serious faults. Nor did these faults escape his observation, for, if there was an eye which saw through and through men, it was the eye of Addison. But, with the keenest observation, and the finest sense of the ridiculous, he had large charity. The feeling with which he looked on most of his humble companions was one of benevolence, slightly tinctured with contempt. He was at perfect ease in their company; he was grateful for their devoted attachment; and he loaded them with benefits. Their veneration for him appears to have exceeded that with which Johnson was regarded by Boswell, or Warburton by Hurd. It was not in the power of adulation to turn such a head, or deprave such a heart, as Addison's. But it must in candour be admitted that he contracted some of the faults which can scarcely be avoided by any person who is so unfortunate as to be the oracle of a small literary coterie.

8. NARRATION

The following excerpt from William Hazlitt's *The Fight* is an excellent example of a swift, vivid narrative paragraph.

When the Gas-man came to himself, the first words he uttered were, "Where am I? What is the matter?" "Nothing is the matter, Tom—you have lost the battle, but you are the bravest man alive." And Jackson whispered to him, "I am collecting a purse for you, Tom." Vain sounds, and unheard at that moment. Neate instantly went up and shook him cordially by the hand, and seeing some old acquaintances, began to flourish with his fists, calling out, "Ah, you always said I couldn't fight—what do you think now?" But all in good humor, and without any appearance of arrogance; only it was evident Bill Neate was pleased that he had won the fight. When it was over, I asked Cribb if he did not think it was a good one. He said, "Pretty well." The carrier-pigeons now mounted into the air, and one of them flew with the news of her husband's victory to the bosom of Mrs. Neate. Alas for Mrs. Hickman!

9. DESCRIPTION

In the following paragraph from Thomas Hardy's *Far From the Madding Crowd*, Gabriel Oak's appearance is described in terms of the clothes he wore.

Since he lived six times as many working days as Sundays, Oak's appearance in his old clothes was peculiarly his own—the mental picture formed by his neighbour in imagining him being always dressed in that way. He wore a low-crowned felt hat, spread out at the base by tight jamming upon the head for security in high winds, and a coat like Dr. Johnson's; his lower extremities being encased in ordinary leather leggings and boots emphatically large, affording to each foot a roomy apartment so constructed that any wearer might stand in a river all day long and know nothing damp—their maker being a conscientious man who endeavoured to compensate for any weakness in his cut by unstinted dimension and solidity.

36 C Suit the length of a paragraph to its purpose.

The length of a paragraph should be determined by (1) the subject (2) the fullness and completeness of development, and

(3) the educational level of the readers. Modern paragraphs are between 100 and 300 words long, but there is no standard length for a paragraph.

Short, scrappy paragraphs should never be written. Paragraphs of one or two sentences should be used only as already explained.

Comparatively short paragraphs are used for slight, simple topics and for larger topics if they are expressed in outline or only in essentials. Short paragraphs are also used in exploratory essays, in essays for the immature, and in swift, terse narration.

Longer paragraphs are used for larger topics and for smaller ones that are specifically and completely developed. Moderately long paragraphs are normally used in formal essays and in expository and narrative prose of leisurely pace.

Excessively long paragraphs may be overloaded with details, or they may include more than one topic. The remedy for the first fault is to remove the unessential details. The remedy for the second fault is to revise the paragraph and limit it to one topic. If the paragraph is excessively long because it includes several aspects of one topic, the paragraph should be logically subdivided.

The beginner can judge the length of paragraphs by the following rough tests:

(1) A paragraph of three or four sentences is probably too short. The thought may be incomplete; details may be omitted; necessary proof or illustration may be lacking.

(2) If a page contains three or more paragraphs, the paragraphs are probably too short and scrappy. Two or more of the paragraphs may belong together. Or all of the paragraphs may require more substance.

(3) A paragraph of a page and a half or more is probably too long. If it is overloaded with details, it should be reduced. If it expresses more than one topic, it should be revised. Otherwise it should be logically subdivided.

SHORT, SCRAPPY PARAGRAPHS

A paragraph is a group of related sentences that develop one thought. A paragraph presents details or illustrations that give substance and meaning to one topic.

[This paragraph omits far too much to be a satisfactory definition of the paragraph.]

An increase in the wages of steel-workers will be inflationary. It will force the steel companies to raise the price of steel. As a result, the prices of many commodities will rise, and our dollar will purchase less than it purchases now.

[This paragraph consists of flat statements without any reasons or explanations. Hence it does not tell the reader why and how a wage rise will be inflationary, nor does it carry any conviction.]

Everyone who has a child in school should join his Parent-Teachers Association. The P.T.A. strives to improve our schools. It helps the pupils, the teachers, and the community.

[Without details to show how the P.T.A. tries to improve the schools and how it is helpful to students, and teachers, and community, this paragraph is weak and ineffectual.]

EXCESSIVELY LONG PARAGRAPH

The fishing in Lake Queequee is excellent. The lake abounds with rock bass, black bass, small-mouth bass, pike, pickerel, yellow perch, white perch, pumpkin seeds or sunfish, bullheads, and eels. The pike, pickerel, and even the yellow perch grow big and gamey. They strike the lure hard and they put up a fight before they are pulled alongside the boat and netted. It is not unusual to land a pickerel measuring thirty inches and weighing four or more pounds. Even the sunfish are big. Some are almost twice the size of a man's hand. When they strike the bait and run with the line, the fisherman has to brace himself and pull hard. The sunfish bite all the time, morning and night and in the blazing afternoon, and in any kind of weather. Anyone can have a thrilling time just catching them, even the children. No sooner does a child drop his line in the water, with a worm, without a worm, than he has a sunfish. In an hour's time he can catch a dozen or more. And the other fish, the pickerel and bass, bite, too, sometimes even for the children. Eventually even a duffer can catch at least one big, gamey fish to display and then to pack in ice and ship home so that the family can admire his skill. Night is the time for eels and bullheads. The hardened fisherman, mindless of mosquitoes and other insects, can always take his outboard motor and go to one of the many coves and there in the shallow water among the weeds and wild rice that grow in abundance, catch eels and bullheads until the break of dawn. Then if he wishes, he can fish for bass and pickerel, and he will probably catch them, too.

> [The point of this paragraph could be made in half the length. It is not necessary, for example, to list all of the kinds of fish in the lake or to give so many details about how the fish are caught and how the fisherman gets to the fishing ground.]

36 D MAKE YOUR PARAGRAPHS UNIFIED.

Unity is as essential in a paragraph as it is in a sentence. Unity means that a paragraph develops only one topic or one aspect of a topic. A paragraph is unified when (1) every sentence contributes to the development of the topic, (2) no sentence fails to advance the topic or introduces another topic, and (3) no sentence necessary to the development of the topic is omitted.

In the following paragraph the remark about the quality of coffee in lunch rooms has nothing to do with the diner's inability to get coffee and a sandwich at the same time. Hence this remark destroys the unity of the paragraph.

In luncheonettes it is almost impossible to order a sandwich and a cup of coffee and to get them at the same time. Usually the sandwich comes first, and the diner waits and waits for the coffee until he can wait no longer. As he is chewing his last bite, the long lost waitress appears with the coffee. *Coffee in lunch rooms is uniformly bad. Either the quality is poor, or the coffee is weak and stale.* Sometimes the coffee is brought first. The diner waits hopefully for the sandwich as the coffee grows cooler and cooler. When the sandwich finally comes, the coffee is cold. Diners have tried every possible means of getting their coffee and sandwich together, but nothing works except luck—once in a blue moon.

The following paragraph by Henry David Thoreau is unified because every sentence, every detail, tells how Thoreau surveyed the country and considered every spot as a possible site for a home.

At a certain season of our life we are accustomed to consider every spot as the possible site of a house. I have thus surveyed the country on every side within a dozen miles of where I live. In imagination I have bought all the farms in succession, for all were to be bought, and I knew their price. I walked over each farmer's premises, tasted his wild apples, discoursed on husbandry with him, took his farm at his price, at any price, mortgaging it to him in my mind; even put a higher price on it,—took everything but a deed of it,—took his word for his deed, for I dearly love to talk,—cultivated it, and him to some extent, I trust, and withdrew when I had enjoyed it long enough, leaving him to carry it on. This experience entitled me to be regarded as a sort of real-estate broker by my friends. Wherever I sat, there I might live, and the landscape radiated from me accordingly. What is a house but a *sedes*, a seat?—better if a country seat. I discovered many a site for a house not likely to be soon improved, which some might have thought too far from the village, but to my eyes the village was too far from it. Well, there I might live, I said; and there I did live, for an hour, a summer, and a winter life; saw how I could let the years run off, buffet the winter through, and see the spring come in. The future inhabitants of this region, wherever they may place their houses, may be sure that they have been anticipated. An afternoon sufficed to lay out the land into orchard, wood-lot, and pasture, and to decide what fine oaks or pines should be left to stand before the door, and whence each blasted tree could be seen to the best advantage; and then I let it lie, fallow perchance, for a man is rich in proportion to the number of things which he can afford to let alone.

36 E Use a topic sentence to state the unifying thought of the paragraph.

The topic sentence states the thought that the rest of the paragraph develops. The topic sentence usually appears at the beginning of the paragraph where it marks the shift from the preceding paragraph and immediately announces the thought now being developed. In some paragraphs the topic sentence appears in the middle, or at the end where it may also act as a summary sentence. Some paragraphs have no topic sentence because the central thought is so obvious that it does not have to be expressed.

The beginner should start each paragraph with a topic sentence. In formulating the topic sentence, he clarifies his thought and fixes the object of the paragraph firmly in mind. He can use the topic sentence as the gauge of what should be included in the paragraph. Details that help to develop the topic sentence should be included; details that do not help, should be excluded. The topic sentence is therefore a prop and control which the beginner needs and one that he may sometimes dispense with only after he has mastered the principles of paragraphing.

Observe how the following topic sentences succinctly express what the paragraph is about:

The mass of men lead lives of quiet desperation. What is called resignation is confirmed desperation. . . . [*Walden,* by Henry David Thoreau]

No young man thinks he will ever die. He may believe that others will, or assent to the doctrine that "all men are mortal" as an abstract proposition, but he is far from bringing it home to himself individually. ["On the Fear of Death," by William Hazlitt]

It is important to remember that, in strictness, there is no such thing as an uneducated man. Take an extreme case. . . . ["A Liberal Education," by Thomas Henry Huxley]

The notions of the beginning and the end of the world entertained by our forefathers are no longer credible. It is very certain that the earth is not the chief body in the natural universe. . . . ["Science and Culture," by Thomas Henry Huxley]

36 F MAKE THE PARAGRAPH COHERENT.

Coherence means natural or logical connection. A paragraph is coherent when (1) its sentences are logically arranged and connected, (2) the logical connection is clear and apparent, (3) the transition from sentence to sentence is easy and natural, and

(4) the reader can see through the interrelationship of details and sentences to the purpose of the paragraph.

Coherence in the paragraph can be achieved in the following ways: (1) by the logical, orderly arrangement of sentences, (2) by the repetition of key words and the use of pronouns to refer to the preceding sentence, (3) by the use of transitional expressions, and (4) by the use of parallel structure (see Sec. 22F).

(1) COHERENCE BY ARRANGEMENT OF SENTENCES

The common ways in which sentences may be logically arranged are illustrated in the following paragraphs. The writer should choose the arrangement or combination of arrangements that best suits his material and his purpose.

TIME ORDER

The sentences of a paragraph may be arranged in order of time. Chronological arrangement is used in narrating action and in explaining a process step by step. In the following paragraph the temporary checks to American vitality are traced chronologically from the depression through World War II and the Korean War to the present.

This vigorous climate for our national vitality has continued until the present. We have had our wars and depressions, but individual enterprise was not seriously challenged until 1929. In the next ten years we learned that progress is a myth, that business does not necessarily grow bigger and better, and that hard work does not always mean success. Then the Second World War taught us some new lessons; so did the Korean War; and so did the Russian earth satellite. Despite these checks, however, our tradition of ambition and aggressiveness remains, and our optimism has been only slightly dimmed.

SPACE ORDER

A paragraph may move from one place to another or from one direction to another. The arrangement of material in space is most useful in descriptive paragraphs. In the paragraph below, the theatre off Broadway is traced from Greenwich Village to the East Side and then to Yorkville in New York City and thence south to Washington, D. C. and west to Los Angeles and San Francisco.

For purpose of contract, Equity has ruled that Off-Broadway is any place outside the area bounded by Fifth and Ninth Avenues and 34th and 56th Streets. In New York, therefore, Off-Broadway is Greenwich Village where the Theatre de Lys, the Cherry Lane, The Provincetown, and other little theatres are located. Off-Broadway is also the lower east side where, among several make-shift theatres, the Phoenix is supreme. Yorktown and the Jan Hus House are also Off-Broadway, and so is any other little theatre outside the area prescribed by Equity. But the spirit of Off-Broadway exists outside of New York. It exists in the theatre in the round in Washington, D. C.; it exists in Dallas, in the smaller groups performing around Los Angeles, and in the Actor's Workshop in San Francisco. Wherever small groups of professional players present plays that for a variety of reasons could not be produced by the so-called commercial theatre, or wherever plays are given experimental productions, there is Off-Broadway.

ORDER OF CLIMAX

The details of a paragraph may be arranged in order of increasing importance. This is an effective arrangement because it builds steadily to a climax. In the following paragraph from Macaulay's essay on Milton, passages of Milton's prose are praised in ascending order as expressing the full power of the English language, as surpassing the finest declamations of Burke, as equaling parts of *Paradise Lost*, and as being an angelic chorus.

It is to be regretted that the prose writings of Milton should, in our time, be so little read. As composition, they deserve the attention of every man who wishes to become acquainted with the full power of the English language. They abound with passages compared with which the finest declamations of Burke sink into insignificance. They are a perfect field of cloth-of-gold. The style is stiff with gorgeous embroidery. Not even in the earlier books of *Paradise Lost* has the great poet ever risen higher than in those parts of his controversial works in which his feelings, excited by conflict, find a vent in bursts of devotional and lyric rapture. It is, to borrow his own majestic language, "a sevenfold chorus of hallelujahs and harping symphonies."

FROM THE FAMILIAR TO THE UNFAMILIAR

The explanatory paragraph below approaches the dialectical law of transformation through familiar facts about water and ice.

Everyone knows that most liquids become solid through freezing. As the temperature of water, for example, is decreased, there is no change in its liquid state. That is, water does not become more gelatinous; it does not become partially solid. Instead, at a certain moment water leaps from the liquid state to the solid one in one bound. This transformation of water into ice is a simple illustration of how, according to dialectics, quantity is transformed into quality and quality into quantity.

FROM THE GENERAL TO THE PARTICULAR

A paragraph may present a general statement and develop it with a number of details. The body of the following paragraph consists of a number of details that support the general statement, expressed in the topic sentence, that Sarzanno held religion in deferential regard.

Sarzanno was not as openly pious as Daniel Drew, but he held religion in deferential regard. At crucial moments he sought its comfort, and in his affluent years he was a ready donor to any religious denomination seeking contributions. During his long and dramatic bout with death and federal agents, he courteously and gratefully accepted a cross from a lay preacher who wished him well and the Sicilian wish for good luck spoken by some of his employees. "I know I need every bit of good luck I can get," he told his biographer. "I'm grabbing everything that comes my way." At different times during his life he swore that he was a Roman Catholic, a Jew, and a Protestant. He was buried as a Jew, but his mother was a devout Catholic, and as she viewed his body for the last time she tried to snatch away the prayer shawl in which he was mantled.

FROM THE PARTICULAR TO THE GENERAL

A paragraph may proceed from a number of details to a general conclusion. In the following paragraph a number of details about the constantly changing nature of things leads to the general conclusion that we never see anything as it really is.

The universe is in an unceasing state of change. The stars move eternally, expanding, cooling, and exploding. The earth itself changes: rivers alter their course, mountains erode, valleys deepen. Life changes through birth, growth, decay, and death. Even desks and houses and boulders are not inert, for at the microscopic level they are whirls of electrons. A desk looks today very much as it did yesterday or a century ago only because the changes in it have been too minute for our coarse perceptions. Matter looks solid to us only because its motion is too rapid or too minute to be felt. Our senses are so extremely limited that we have to use instruments such as microscopes, telescopes, seismographs, etc. to detect occurrences which our unaided senses are powerless to detect. Today even children know that there are vibrations we cannot hear and configurations we cannot see. Therefore it is ludicrous to think that we ever perceive anything as it really is.

(2) COHERENCE BY THE USE OF KEY WORDS
AND THE REPETITION OF PRONOUNS

The repetition of important words in a paragraph keeps the reader constantly aware of the subject and binds the sentences together in a tightly unified whole. The repetition of pronouns helps to achieve the same effect and to make the thought flow smoothly from sentence to sentence. Note how the following paragraph is bound together by the repetitions that are woven through it.

The disparagers of *culture* make *its motive curiosity;* sometimes, indeed, they make *its motive* mere exclusiveness and *vanity.* The *culture* which is supposed to plume *itself* on a smattering of Greek and Latin is a *culture* which is begotten by nothing so intellectual as *curiosity;* it is valued out of sheer *vanity* and ignorance or else as an engine of social and class distinction; separating *its* holders, like a badge or title, from other people who have not got *it.* No *serious* man would call this *culture,* or attach any value to it, as *culture,* at all. To find the real ground for the very different estimate which *serious* people will set upon *culture,* we must find some *motive* for *culture* in the terms of which may lie a real ambiguity; and such a *motive* the word *curiosity* gives us. ["Sweetness and Light," by Matthew Arnold]

(3) COHERENCE BY TRANSITIONAL EXPRESSIONS

By showing the relationship between thoughts, transitional expressions help the reader to move from detail to detail and from sentence to sentence with a sense of direction and continuity. In addition to the repetition of key words and pronouns, coherence can be achieved by the use of the following transitional expressions:

Addition: in addition, again, moreover, further, furthermore, finally, lastly, at last, in conclusion, first, second, etc.

Contrast: but, however, yet, still, nevertheless, on the other hand, after all, for all of that, on the contrary, notwithstanding, it is true

Comparison: similarly, likewise, in like manner

Purpose: to this end, with this object, for this purpose

Result: accordingly, thus, consequently, hence, therefore, wherefore, thereupon

Emphasis: in fact, indeed, in any event, certainly

Example: for example, for instance, thus, in this manner

Summary: in brief, on the whole, in sum, to sum up, in fine

Time: at once, immediately, while, meanwhile, at length, in the meantime, at the same time, in the end, in the interim, when, as, while, etc.

Place: near, beyond, opposite to, adjacent to, at the same place, here, there, etc.

In the following paragraph from "On The Physical Basis of Life," by Thomas Henry Huxley the transitional expressions are italicized.

And what is this dire necessity and "iron" law under which men groan? *Truly*, most gratuitously invented bugbears. I suppose if there be an "iron" law, it is that of gravitation; *and* if there be a physical necessity, it is that a stone, unsupported, must fall to the ground. *But* what is all we really know, and can know, about the latter phenomenon? *Simply*, that in all human experience stones have fallen to the ground under these conditions; that we have not the smallest reason for believing that any stone so circumstanced will not fall to the ground; *and* that we have, *on the contrary*, every reason to believe that it will so fall. It is very convenient to indicate that all the conditions of a belief have been fulfilled in this case, by calling the statement that unsupported stones will fall to the ground, "a law of nature." *But when, as commonly happens*, we change *will* [sic] into *must* [sic] we introduce an idea of necessity which *most assuredly* does not lie in the observed facts, *and* has no warranty that I can discover anywhere. *For my part*, I utterly repudiate and anathematize the intruder. Fact I know, *and* law I know; *but* what is this Necessity, save an empty shadow of my mind's throwing?

36 G Provide transition between paragraphs.

In addition to providing transition from sentence to sentence within a paragraph, the writer must also provide transition from paragraph to paragraph. Transition between paragraphs can be achieved by the use of a transitional expression or sentence. Transition from one major division of a composition to another may be achieved by the use of a transitional paragraph. A summarizing paragraph may also be used to show the relationship between the preceding and following parts of an essay.

TRANSITION BETWEEN PARAGRAPHS

As a matter of fact, although few things are spoken of with more fearful whisperings than this prospect of death, few have less influence on conduct under healthy circumstances. . . .

On the other hand, religion has its own enlargement, and an enlargement, not of tumult, but of peace. . . .

You will see what I mean by the parallel of bodily health. . . .

Let us then put aside the scientific use of words, when we are to speak of language and literature. . . .

We now come to the Royalists. . . .

TRANSITIONAL PARAGRAPHS

And now, what is the ultimate fate, and what the origin, of the matter of life? ["On the Physical Basis of Life," by Thomas Henry Huxley]

The foregoing remarks are intended merely as a prelude to a narrative I am about to lay before the public, of one of the most memorable instances of this infatuation of gain to be found in the whole history of commerce. I allude to the famous Mississippi bubble. It is a matter that has passed into proverb, and become a phrase in every one's mouth, yet of which not one merchant in ten has probably a distinct idea. I have therefore thought that an authentic account of it would be interesting and salutary, at the present moment, when we are suffering under the effects of a severe access of the credit system, and just recovering from one of its ruinous delusions. [From *Wolfert's Roost and Other Papers*, by Washington Irving]

Having dwelt so much on this first and leading error in respect to opium, I shall notice very briefly a second and a third; which are, that the elevation of spirits produced by opium is necessarily followed by a proportionate depression, and that the natural and even immediate consequence of opium is torpor and stagnation, animal and mental. The first of these errors I shall content myself with simply denying, assuring my reader, that for ten years, during which I took opium at intervals, the day succeeding to that on which I allowed myself the luxury was always a day of good spirits. [*The Pleasures of Opium*, by Thomas De Quincey]

·THE WRITER'S APPROACH TO HIS SUBJECT

From the novice with something to write comes the anguished cry: "How do I go about it?" Unfortunately for the novice there is no universal formula for writing. How a writer should go about his task depends on his subject, his purpose, and his readers. Every projected piece of writing is a new problem that requires its own solution. Nevertheless, there are general procedures and rules that apply to almost any kind of prose. If the beginner is guided by them, he should be able to produce an acceptable piece of writing.

The prerequisites for good writing are time and effort. The beginner should therefore be prepared to work hard, and he should not attempt to complete a paper in one sitting. Instead he should divide his task into logical steps and take them a few at a time until the work is done. With a simple, familiar subject the writer might, for example, determine his purpose and gather his material in one session, plan the paper in the second, and write and re-write it in the third. More difficult subjects obviously require more time and effort and therefore more periods of work. The number of periods the writer devotes to his paper should, of course, be determined by the topic and by the writer's ability and temperament.

The advantages of writing a paper in easy, logical steps are obvious. Being spread over a number of periods, the task becomes less burdensome and painful. The writer brings a fresh, clear mind to each session. Each stage of the preparation leads to the next and makes it easier. In the intervals the writer gains perspective on the work already done and is therefore able to judge and improve it. The improvement is cumulative, and the result is a better paper.

37 SELECT AND ADAPT A SUBJECT WITH CARE.

All writing begins with a subject. One may be required to write about a specific subject or one of several subjects, or he may, of course, be free to choose any subject he likes. If he is fortunate enough to have free choice, he should be able to make the most of his opportunity, for success in writing depends, to a considerable extent, on an appropriate subject. But even if one must write on an assigned subject, he can lighten his task and increase his chances of success by adapting the subject to his own interests and sphere of knowledge. The first step to the successful completion of an assignment in writing, therefore, is to choose or adapt the subject wisely.

37 A Choose a subject that interests you.

The advantages of an interesting subject should be obvious. It makes the task of writing easier and pleasanter than it would otherwise be. An interesting subject induces an enthusiasm that the writer will in all likelihood communicate to the reader. The reverse is, of course, true. If the writer is bored, his writing will be leaden, and the reader will, in turn, be bored. Only a skillful writer can feign an interest and enthusiasm that he does not have.

The subject should interest the writer. Generally speaking, he should not worry about the subject being of interest to others. Chances are that any subject of interest to one individual is also of interest to many others. And even if a reader finds the subject itself dull, he may yet enjoy the work because of the writer's enthusiasm. We have all had the experience of being fascinated by someone else's enjoyment of something that we do not like. "I wouldn't care for that," we say to ourselves, "but I can understand why he does."

There are, of course, numerous occasions when the writer must be careful to select a subject that will interest his readers. Whenever one writes for a specific group or a specific occasion, he must select his subject accordingly. Of course, the ideal subject is one that suits both the occasion and the writer.

37 B Choose a subject that you know about or are willing to learn about.

To write about a subject one must, of course, know about it. Knowledge is the substance of which writing is made. One can no more write an article without knowledge than he can knit a sock without yarn. In order to give his writing substance and conviction the writer must have facts and opinions based upon facts. Knowledge of a subject gives a writer confidence and direction, whereas ignorance causes him to fumble and grope. If the writer is ignorant, his writing will be worthless. If he is uninformed and vague, his writing will be uninformed and vague. Even minor omissions and mistakes are likely to invalidate the entire paper. Knowledge of the subject does not guarantee successful writing, but it is a necessary ingredient. Without it, failure is certain.

The student of writing should, therefore, select a subject that he already knows or that he is willing to learn more about. He can supplement his knowledge in the usual ways: by examining the subject, or reading about it, or by questioning others, or by a combination of these methods. He can also limit his discussion of a subject to a logical part that he is already familiar with. The matter of limiting and adapting a subject is discussed in the next section.

In deciding what to write, the beginner should not reject familiar subjects because they are, he thinks, commonplace and dull. Usually it is not the subject but the treatment that is dull. Familiar subjects, those chosen from school, family, work, and social life, are the ones that everyone can write about most intimately. And they are subjects that everyone likes to read about, for the recognition of the familiar is one of the greatest pleasures in reading.

On the other hand, the beginner should not write about the bizarre and the adventurous unless he has experienced them. Otherwise, his writing will lack detail and verisimilitude. At best it will be vague, generalized, and totally unconvincing and uninteresting.

37 C   Choose a subject that you can write about with honesty of purpose.

A writer should always write for a purpose with which he is in accord. He should express honest convictions and judgments. He should not pretend to like things or to believe in causes merely because he thinks that the reader expects him to. If he cannot write honestly about a subject, he should not write about it at all.

Moral reasons aside, writing dishonestly is writing against the grain. An experienced writer can make a case for something he does not believe in because he has mastered the tools of expression and can manipulate words and ideas with dexterity. Any student of writing has all he can do to determine his opinions and express them clearly. He must first be able to express his own side of a question before attempting to write on other sides of it.

37 D   Limit the subject in scope.

The writer should select a subject that can be adequately developed in the number of words at his disposal. If the subject is so slight that it must be padded, it should be rejected. If a broad subject cannot be logically reduced to the required limits, it, too, should be rejected.

Most subjects can be limited in scope. Some of the more usual ways of limiting a subject are listed below and are, for the sake of concreteness, illustrated with the subject of trade unionism.

TIME

The Origin of Trade Unionism
Trade Unionism in the Depression

PLACE

Trade Unionism in Salt Lake City
Trade Unionism in my Shop

COMPONENT PARTS

Trade Unionism in the Automotive Industry
My Union Local

ORGANIZATION

The Union Local
The Shop Steward

MODES OF OPERATION

The Strike as a Union Weapon
The Union Welfare Fund

DEFINITION

What Is Trade Unionism?
The A.F. of L.—C.I.O.

CAUSE AND EFFECT

Why Labor Organized
Unions and Higher Wages

"The Origin of Trade Unionism" would require a monograph
or a long essay, depending on the fullness of treatment. At the
other end of the scale "Why My Shop Should Organize" might
be developed in a thousand words or less.

The writer may, of course, apply several limitations to his
subject. A factual account of the Boston police strike, for example, limits the subject of trade unionism to an impartial narration of a particular strike action at a definite time in a specific
place. "Why My Shop Should Organize" is limited to a definite
time and place and, perhaps, to a few salient reasons why, under

the circumstances, a specific group of workers should join a union.

It is not even necessary to cover a limited subject completely. The writer may, for example, further limit it by dealing with only the most important points and omitting the others. In George Bernard Shaw's *St. Joan,* for example, the Bishop of Beauvais reduces the indictment of Joan from sixty-four counts to twelve, saying that if she were tried on a great many issues she might escape on the great main issue of heresy. The great main issues are frequently enough to establish a case or make a point; the minor issues are often superfluous and are, sometimes, injurious because they seem to dilute the argument.

37 E   Adapt the subject to your own sphere of interest and knowledge.

The writer should adapt his subject to his own sphere of interest and knowledge. If, for example, his general subject is civil defense, he can write about the provisions for civil defense in his community or his shop. If he has a broader knowledge of the subject, he might write about the inadequacies of the program and suggest improvements, or he might, from his investigations, oppose the program in whole or in part.

Many subjects can be adapted in this manner. They can be discussed on the immediate and even personal level of home, school, or shop, or they can be discussed on a higher and more general level. No matter what the subject, the writer should discuss it concretely in an area with which he is familiar. He should, in a manner of speaking, cut the subject to his own size and tackle it on his home ground.

38   DETERMINE YOUR FUNDAMENTAL PURPOSE IN WRITING.

The first thing a writer should do after selecting and adapting the subject is to determine his fundamental purpose. Almost any subject can be developed in a number of different ways. How it is developed depends on the writer's purpose. Take, for example, "An Account of Judge Mission's Record in Office." The purpose of this account might be to persuade people to re-elect the Judge or to defeat him. Or the purpose might be to present an impartial statement of the Judge's record so that the voter can decide for himself. And there might be still other purposes such as to state why the President should appoint him to the Supreme Court, or why Harvard should give him an honorary degree, or why he should be impeached and disbarred.

Since most subjects can be treated in different ways, the writer must decide at the outset what he wants to accomplish. Otherwise he is likely to vacillate between two or more goals and thus, through irresolution, produce a confused and pointless piece of writing.

On the other hand, if the writer states his purpose clearly, he knows what he wants to accomplish and he has a lodestone to keep him on his course. With his purpose as a guide, the writer can decide what material to include and what to exclude because it is irrelevant or contradictory. He can decide what tone and mood to adopt, in what order to arrange his material, and where to place his emphasis. The guiding purpose is, in fact, the device a writer uses to bring every aspect of his writing into focus.

It is therefore good practice for the beginner to state his purpose in the following manner:

I am writing an account of Judge Elton W. Mission's record in office to persuade the voters to re-elect him.

I am writing this letter to persuade Johnson and Duckwith, Inc. to take back the Chinese rug I purchased and to refund my money.

I am telling this story about my narrow escape from death in the crash landing of an airplane in order to make the reader's blood run cold.

I am explaining how to cure meat so that the reader can, by following my instructions, cure his own meat.

39 GATHER AND RECORD YOUR MATERIAL.

Once the writer has determined his purpose, he should gather and record the substance necessary to express it in writing. Material may be obtained from the following sources:

(1) From the writer's own fund of knowledge.

From his own mind the writer should cull every bit of pertinent information and jot it down, point by point. If the writer is familiar with the subject, he may not have to go elsewhere for material. If his own knowledge is not sufficient, however, he must supplement it with information from other sources.

(2) From observation and interrogation

The writer can obviously increase his knowledge of a subject by observation and interrogation. If he is writing about the condition or operation of something, for example, he can watch and examine it for himself. If he is writing about how people are affected by something or what they think about it, he can observe them and question a representative number about the matter.

(3) From the literature on the subject

The most obvious source of information about a subject is what others have written about it. Newspapers, magazines, house organs, technical journals, and books are unfailing sources of information. To find the available information the writer should use the following aids:

(1) The articles and bibliographies in standard dictionaries, encyclopedias, and histories.

(2) *The Times Index*

(3) *The Readers Guide to Periodical Literature*

(4) Bibliographies of the various subjects

(5) Subject entries in the card catalogue of the library

(6) The librarian

40   MAKE A PLAN OF YOUR WRITING.

All writing should be planned in advance. Planning a subject is thinking about it systematically. The plan is the writer's diagram; it is as necessary to the writer as the blueprint to the machinist or the pattern to the dressmaker. Most bad writing is planless writing, writing that is aimless, confused, and even self-contradictory. Without taking thought, the writer sits down and writes, or tries to. It never occurs to him that he should think before he writes. Yet he would make elaborate plans for spending a day at the beach or constructing a radiator cover. To most people writing is a mystery. It requires divinely inspired talent; either one has it or he does not and there is nothing he can do about it. This is a mistaken notion. The ability to write effectively is no more mysterious than any other skill. It can be acquired by thought and practice. An essay and a radiator cover are made in the same way: by taking thought, making a plan, gathering the material, and then executing the work. Neither the radiator cover nor the essay may be a work of art, but they will be serviceable. And, of course, one will do better with practice.

To the writer the plan has obvious advantages. It means that he has analyzed his subject completely, patterned his material, and determined the following things:

(1) his fundamental purpose in writing

(2) the major parts of his subject

(3) the order in which the major parts should be arranged

(4) the substance to develop each of the major parts

(5) the arrangement of the substance in each of the major parts

(6) the subdivisions and the substance and arrangement of them

The author with a plan has thought his subject through. He knows exactly what he wants to say and how to go about saying it. He knows where to begin, how to proceed from point to point, and where to end. He has built a skeleton and now needs only to cover it with a fabric of words.

The plan simplifies the actual process of writing. Having planned his work, the writer does not now have to think about what to say, how to say it, and what to say next. Unlike the juggler who has to keep several objects in the air at the same time, the writer is now free to concentrate on only one problem —how to express his thoughts in words. He will not make false starts and contradictory statements, wander up blind alleys, or go around in circles. He will be able to write more quickly and more correctly. Solecisms in writing—incomplete and fused sentences, mixed and illogical sentences, disagreements—frequently result from confusion rather than ignorance. By eliminating the confusion, the plan reduces the number of solecisms, for the writer who has planned his work properly is not trapped into error. Having completed the draft, he will have to revise it, but he will not have to reorganize and rewrite it because of illogical organization or vital omissions.

All writing therefore requires forethought, and all but the simplest writing requires a written plan. The scope of the plan will depend on the subject. It should be obvious that the larger and more complex the subject is, the more detailed the plan must be.

The process of planning and writing an essay can be illustrated with the subject of our water supply. Let us assume that the writer has decided upon his purpose and expressed it as follows: to give children an easy, general explanation of how we get our drinking water.

From his knowledge of the subject and perhaps from further study of it, the writer jots down the following items:

1. The reservoirs and watersheds
2. The protection of the watersheds
3. The prohibition of bathing, boating, etc.
4. The screens to filter the water
5. The ways the dams are constructed
6. The water tower in the stream

7. The pumping of water to the purifying station
8. How these pumps are powered
9. The cost of operating the pumps
10. The need for more reservoirs as a protection against water shortage
11. The huge tanks in the purifying station
12. The use of chemicals to purify the water
13. The settling of the impurities
14. The condition of the water at the end of this purifying process
15. The pumping of the water to another purifying station
16. The appearance of the hall
17. The use of sand and gravel to purify the water here
18. The central passageway
19. The reservoirs on the sides
20. How these filters operate
21. The layers of sand and gravel
22. What happens in this filtering plant
23. The checking of the filtering operations here
24. The corrective measures taken in the purifying station
25. The laboratory analysis of the water
26. The training required of the chemists
27. The equipment of the laboratory
28. The addition of purifying chemicals—chlorine
29. The pumping station
30. The underground pipes
31. The leading of water to the pumping station
32. The branching of the large pipes into networks of smaller ones
33. The laying and maintenance of this network of pipes
34. The pumping of water into houses by huge pumps in the pumping stations
35. The emergency water tower
36. How the water tower operates
37. What the water towers look like

Scrutinizing these items, the writer notes that despite his controlling purpose he has included irrelevant material. He therefore eliminates the following items because they are not central to his purpose or would make his explanation too detailed and technical.

5. The ways the dams are constructed
8. How these pumps are powered
9. The cost of operating these pumps
10. The need for more reservoirs as a protection against water shortage
26. The training required of the chemists
27. The equipment of the laboratory
33. The laying and maintenance of these pipes

The writer also eliminates the following items because they are repetitious:

3. The prohibition of bathing, boating, etc.—because it repeats item 2, the protection of the watersheds
21. The layers of sand and gravel—because it repeats item 17, the use of sand and gravel to purify the water
22. What happens in the filtering plant—because it repeats item 20, how the filters operate
29. The pumping station—because it is sufficiently covered by item 31

Next, the writer scrutinizes the remaining items to see that they are in the step-by-step sequence required by the general process he is explaining. Since some of the items are not in proper order, he re-arranges and re-numbers the list as follows:

1. The reservoirs
2. The protection of the reservoirs
3. The water tower in the reservoir
4. The screens to filter the water
5. The pumping of the water to the purifying station
6. The huge tanks in the purifying station
7. The settling of impurities in the tanks
8. The use of chemicals to aid the settling process
9. The condition of the water at the end of the purifying process

10. The appearance of the hall
11. The central passageway
12. The reservoirs on the sides
13. The layers of sand and gravel
14. How the water is filtered
15. The checking of these filtering operations
16. The corrective measures taken
17. The laboratory analysis of the water
18. The addition of purifying chemicals—chlorine
19. The leading of water to the pumping station
20. The huge underground pipes
21. The branching of the large pipes into a network of smaller ones
22. The pumping of the water into the smaller pipes and up into the houses
23. The emergency water towers
24. How these emergency towers work

Although the items are now arranged in proper sequence, they are not arranged logically. There is no distinction between major and minor items; the relationship between the whole and its parts is not indicated. Consequently the writer now organizes the items to indicate these divisions and relationships.

I. The reservoir and its protection
   A. The prohibition of bathing, boating, fishing, etc.
   B. The patrolman to prevent violations

II. The water tower in the reservoir
   A. Its underwater windows
   B. The screens to filter the filth
   C. The pumping of the water to the purifying station

III. The purifying station with its huge tanks
   A. The settling of impurities in the water
   B. The use of chemical to aid the settling process
   C. The condition of the water at the end of this process

IV. The next purifying station
   A. The hall

1. The central passageway with its tile floor
2. The reservoirs on the sides
3. The layers of sand and gravel
   B. How the water is filtered
   C. The checking of the filtering process and the correct-
      ive measures taken
   D. The laboratory analysis of the water and the addition
      of chlorine
   V. The pumping station
   A. The leading of water to it
   B. The pumping of water into huge underground pipes
   VI. The network of smaller pipes in the cities
   A. The conduction of the water into these smaller pipes
   B. The pumping of the water up into the houses
   VII. The emergency water tower and how it works.

This outline is a topic outline. The writer may, if he wishes, write a sentence outline; that is, he may express the major and minor items in sentences rather than in phrases and clauses. Some writers use paragraph outlines which consist of the topic sentence of each paragraph in the essay. The kind of outline the writer makes is of little importance. The important thing is that the writer plan his essay before writing.

41 WRITE THE ESSAY FROM THE PLAN.

Once the writer has made a plan and checked it carefully, he should follow it in writing his essay. He should write a series of coherent paragraphs covering all of the items in the outline in their order of appearance. If he thinks of a better arrangement while he is writing, he should not hesitate to make the change, for an outline is intended as a guide and not as a straitjacket. After an introductory paragraph the following explanation of how we get our drinking water follows the plan item by item.

THE WATER IN OUR SINK

When we turn on the faucet, water gushes out. Have you ever wondered where the water comes from and how it gets to the tap? And have you ever wondered what makes it so clean and pure?

Our water comes from lakes and streams. Some of them are natural bodies of water, and some of them are made by dams which force the water to collect in large reservoirs. These reservoirs are very carefully protected in order to keep them clean. No one is allowed to fish or swim in them or even to boat on most of them. There are guards to enforce these prohibitions and to see that the water is not contaminated in any other way. The guards prevent anyone from washing clothes in the water and dumping refuse in it. If the guards discover any violation, they report it to the authorities and arrest the violators.

In the reservoirs there is a huge underwater tower two or more stories high with windows through which the water runs. On the outside of these windows are coarse screens and on the inside are finer ones. These screens filter out twigs, leaves, paper, and other coarse objects, including fish, both live and dead ones. The filtered water then runs into a pumping station and is pumped to a purifying station.

The purifying station contains huge tanks in which the water moves very slowly. When brooks and rivers run swiftly, their currents carry off twigs, leaves, silt and other heavy matter, but when water runs slowly, the impurities sink to the bottom. This settling process is aided by chemicals which form large, white flakes upon the surface of the water. As these flakes sink, they carry impurities to the bottom with them.

When the water runs out of these tanks, it is only a bit cloudy and even seems to be pure. But if you were to examine it under a microscope, you would see thousands of objects swarming in it. These objects are bacteria. Since some bacteria are harmful, they must be removed so that they cannot make people ill.

In order that these bacteria can be removed, the water is pumped into another purifying station. This place is a large, light hall with a floor of white tile. Down the center of the hall runs a passageway; on both sides of it are small, square pools. The bottom of these pools is covered with slits through which the water runs out. Over these slits is a layer of gravel and then a thick layer of sand. The water seeps through the sand and gravel, but the bacteria and other dirt remain.

Of course, the bacteria are much smaller than a grain of sand, and the spaces between two grains of sand might just as well be an open door as far as they are concerned. What, then, keeps them inside the door?

This is what happens. As the water seeps through, it covers each grain of sand with a film of tiny water plants and bacteria. Other bacteria stick to this film as they are about to pass between the grains of sand. Strange as it seems, the bacteria themselves help to clear the water of bacteria.

While the water is being filtered, a man keeps watch. Wearing clean overalls and felt slippers, he walks up and down the passageway. He sees to it that the water is seeping through the sand in the pools at the proper rate. If the water seeps too slowly, the sand is dirty. Then the man closes some pipes and opens others. As a result, the water no longer runs through the dirty pond, but is sent into a clean one.

The water that leaves the hall seems clean, but it still contains some bacteria. In the purifying station is a laboratory where technicians examine the water to make sure that it is free of harmful bacteria. If any are detected, the director of the purifying station is immediately informed. He directs the river guards to find out why the water is contaminated and where.

In order to kill any bacteria that remain in the water, a technician adds a yellow poison called chlorine. The amount added is so small that the people cannot smell or taste it when they drink the water. But even such a small amount is enough to kill the bacteria.

Now that the water is thoroughly pure, it goes to the next station, a pumping station. In this station huge pumps force the water through large underground pipes. These pipes stretch for many miles and carry the water into the city. In the city the big pipe branches into many smaller pipes. The large stream of water is thus broken into many smaller streams which flow in all directions. Imprisoned in the pipes, these little streams flow into the houses and up to the top floors.

If you open the tap, the water gushes out. It flows with such force because large pumps at the pumping stations are constantly exerting pressure on it and forcing it through the pipes. Sometimes these pumps break and must be repaired. But even then the houses are not left without water.

For emergencies like this, water is kept in water towers. They are very big with round houses on the top and a narrow stairway winding up them. Inside there is a huge tank filled

with water. The water tank is like a pond suspended high above the houses and trees. The
tower is built so high in order that the water
can be forced down with pressure great enough
to force it up to the top floors of buildings.
And so there is always clean, pure water for
cooking and drinking, and even for bathing.

41 A   Check the first draft of the essay carefully.

After the writer has completed the first draft of his essay, he
should read it critically and make all of the necessary revisions
and corrections. A draft has been properly edited when it meets
the following conditions:

(1) It corresponds to the plan, except for improvements made
in the course of composition.

(2) It is free of errors in grammar and structure.

(3) It is free from errors in spelling, punctuation, and mechanics.

(4) It is clear and logical.

(5) It flows smoothly from paragraph to paragraph.

While revising the draft, the writer should read it aloud or
have it read to him, for the ear often detects errors which the
eye has missed. If the writer is uncertain, he may also seek the
advice of someone who is competent to judge his work as a
whole and to call attention to weaknesses and errors in it. However, the writer should accept suggestions only if he is convinced
of their validity, and he should make the suggested changes
himself. Anyone who is learning to write can profit by intelligent
criticism, but not by having his work done for him.

41 B   Write the final version from the revised draft.

After the writer has revised his draft to incorporate all of the
necessary changes, he should write his final version. He should

then compare it with the draft to make sure that he has copied correctly and incorporated every change. Once again he should read the final version to be sure that it is free of error.

To be acceptable a paper must be neat and legible, satisfy the established rules for the preparation of manuscripts (see p. 167) and contain no more than three corrections on a page. Corrections must be neat and unobtrusive. The writer should understand that an attractive paper commends itself to the reader.

42 BEGIN AND END THE PAPER PROPERLY.

A paper should have a beginning, a middle, and an end. It should begin where the subject opens and end where the subject closes. It should begin by commanding the reader's attention and end when the argument is complete and before it is nullified or the reader is bored.

42 A Write an opening that is suitable to the article and the anticipated audience.

Although there is no standard way to begin an essay, the opening must at least introduce the topic. One must not be expected to infer the topic as he reads or to learn of it from the title. It is a convention that all articles must begin as if the title did not exist. An essay should not begin as follows:

EARLY MARRIAGES

Mother was twenty-six when she married father, and grandmother was married at twenty-four. But my sister Beth now wants to get married and she is seventeen.

Although the title of this essay announces the topic, the opening does not. From the first three sentences the reader can merely infer that the essay is about marriage in general. A better opening would be:

Early Marriages

Today early marriages are in vogue. My sister Beth is seventeen and she wants to get married. At seventeen and a half her friend Sally is already married and pregnant. But mother was twenty-six when she married father, and grandmother was married at twenty-four.

Short essays and essays of moderate length on subjects of general interest do not, as a rule, require a formal introduction. The opening should introduce the topic and arouse the reader's interest. The art of the brief, striking introduction is illustrated by Charles Lamb's "A Chapter on Ears." The opening paragraph is:

I have no ear.

Hazlitt opens his essay "On The Fear of Death" swiftly:

Perhaps the best cure for the fear of death is to reflect that life has a beginning as well as an end.

Hazlitt also employs a swift, striking introductory sentence in "Whether Genius Is Conscious of Its Powers?":

No really great man ever thought himself so.

An introductory device that is frequently used to pique the reader's curiosity is the question. The model essay "The Water in Our Sink" in this section begins:

When we turn on the faucet, water gushes out. Have you ever wondered where the water comes from and how it gets to our sink? And have you ever wondered what makes it so pure and clean?

An essay explaining the origin and nature of the wind might also begin with questions and interesting statements as follows:

Do you think that invisible creatures exist only in fairy tales? Then look up in the sky. See the white clouds floating way up there? What is pushing them? The Invisible One. When it crosses a field, the wheat bows low to it; when it passes through a forest, the trees bend down their heads. In autumn it whirls the dry leaves down the street; in summer it beats up the dust and tosses it into people's eyes.

You've surely guessed what it is by now. It is the wind, the invisible current of air that moves over the earth.

Another effective introductory device is the anecdote. Wilhelm Friedrich van Anspach's essay "The Early Flowering of Mozart's Genius" begins as follows:

> One day in Mozart's fourth year, Andreas Schactner, court trumpeter at Salzburg, accompanied Leopold Mozart to his home. There in his father's study they found young Wolfgang writing with a pen. He was writing a concerto for the clavier. Looking at it Schactner saw a daub of notes over dried ink-blots. He and Leopold laughed at the apparent nonsense. But then Leopold began to note the theme and the composition. Tears of wonder and delight filled his eyes.
>
> "See, Herr Schactner," he said, "how proper and logical it is, but it's useless because it is too difficult for anyone to play."
>
> "That's why it's a concerto," Wolfgang insisted. "One must practice it until he can play it." Then he played it, but only enough to show what he intended. And this was, as I have already said, when he was only four years old.

Some articles require a formal introduction. A formal introduction does more than announce the topic; it explains the purpose, scope, and method of the article. Formal introductions are used for long and complex reports and for investigations in which the reader requires preparation and guidance. Formal introductions may also serve to explain the pertinence of a topic and to justify essays on subjects which a reader, for a variety of reasons, might think ought not be discussed.

In his essay on "The Physical Basis of Life," Thomas Henry Huxley begins with a formal introduction because the discussion is somewhat technical and because he believes his ideas to be novel and somewhat shocking:

> In order to make the title of this discourse generally intelligible, I have translated the term "Protoplasm," which is the scientific name of the substance of which I am about to speak, by the words "the physical basis of life." I suppose that, to many, the idea that there

is such a thing as a physical basis, or matter, of life may be novel—so widely spread is the conception of life as a something which works through matter, but is independent of it; and even those who are aware that matter and life are inseparably connected, may not be prepared for the conclusion plainly suggested by the phrase, "*the physical basis of life*," that there is some one kind of matter which is common to all living beings, and that their endless diversities are bound together by a physical, as well as an ideal, unity. In fact, when first apprehended, such a doctrine as this appears almost shocking to common sense.

To explain why and under what circumstances *Walden* was written, and also to anticipate the charge of immodesty, Henry David Thoreau wrote a long introduction to his work:

When I wrote the following pages, or rather the bulk of them, I lived alone, in the woods, a mile from any neighbor, in a house which I had built myself, on the shore of Walden Pond, in Concord, Massachusetts, and earned my living by the labor of my hands only. I lived there two years and two months. At present I am a sojourner in civilized life again.

I should not obtrude my affairs so much on the notice of my readers if very particular inquiries had not been made by my townsmen concerning my mode of life, which some would call impertinent, though they do not appear to me at all impertinent, but, considering the circumstances, very natural and pertinent. Some have asked what I got to eat; if I did not feel lonesome; if I was not afraid; and the like. Others have been curious to learn what portion of my income I devoted to charitable purposes; and some, who have large families, how many poor children I maintained. I will therefore ask those of my readers who feel no particular interest in me to pardon me if I undertake to answer some of these questions in this book. In most books, the *I*, or first person, is omitted; in this it will be retained; that, in respect to egotism, is the main difference. We commonly do not remember that it is, after all, always the first person that is speaking. I should not talk so much about myself if there were anybody else whom I knew as well. Unfortunately, I am confined to this theme by the narrowness of my experience. Moreover, I, on my side, require of every writer, first or last, a simple and sincere account of his own life, and not merely what he has heard of other men's lives; some such account as he would send to his kindred from a distant land; for if he has lived sincerely it must have been in a distant land to me. Perhaps these pages are more particularly addressed to poor students. As for the rest of my readers, they will accept such portions as apply to them. I trust that none will stretch the seams in putting on the coat, for it may do good service to him whom it fits.

The first paragraph of Harold S. Friedburg's article "You Can Take Good Pictures" explains the purpose and the method:

Even you can take good pictures. You can take good pictures without an expensive camera and elaborate equipment. You can take good pictures without first taking a course in photography. Let me tell you how. First I will tell you what equipment to buy. Then I will explain what a good picture is, and finally I will tell you how to take one. At the end of this article I will give a succinct list of instructions. Keep it with you, follow it, and you can't go wrong.

42 B As a rule, do not end a paper with a formal conclusion.

For most essays a formal conclusion is unnecessary. When the argument has been completed, the paper should end on a tonic note of finality.

A formal conclusion is used in a lengthy, complex exposition to state conclusions and to summarize points which the reader may have forgotten. In shorter and less formal exposition, however, a summary is superfluous.

Here is the end of Hazlitt's essay "On the Fear of Death."

If we merely wish to continue our headstrong humours and tormenting passions, we had better begone at once; and if we only cherish a fondness for existence according to the good we derive from it, the pang we feel at parting with it will not be very severe.

42 C Do not begin a narrative long before the incident being narrated.

In narrating an incident the writer should begin with the circumstances in which it occurred and the events immediately preceding it. He should not begin with unnecessary explanations or remote and inconsequential events. An indirect or longwinded approach bores the reader and destroys the impact of the story. Furthermore, the writer may get lost in a maze of inconsequential details or exhaust himself before he has narrated the climax of his story.

Suppose that one is telling how he and his wife were nearly drowned when they rowed into the ship's channel at Gloucester, Massachusetts, and their boat was swamped by a passing freighter. This story should probably begin with their taking the boat out. The writer can then concentrate on how, unthinkingly, they rowed into the channel and on the ensuing events together with their emotional reactions to them. The story should not begin with an explanation of why the couple decided to vacation in Gloucester. Nor is it necessary to say that on the preceding evening a guest at their hotel suggested the excursion, or even that they were eager to get out on the water because they had been kept indoors for three days by a northeaster.

Some representative beginnings:

(1) At four o'clock in the afternoon we drove up to the gate of the Rocky National Park. Since the hour was late, I asked the ranger if we had time to cross Big Ridge into Estes before dark. [For an account of a harrowing drive over Big Ridge in a blinding snow storm.]

(2) When I was ushered to my place at the table, my heart sank. The woman at my left was Miss Tompkins. Ironsides Tompkins, the scourge of the Personnel Department! [For an incident leading to the revelation that the reviled Miss Tompkins is a woman of intelligence and charm.]

(3) "I just talked to Tom on the 'phone, Ma," Iris said. "He'll be over this evening."

Mrs. Sears laid her newspaper aside. "Like last Thursday?" she asked.

"Oh, he'll come all right. I told him you and Pa'd be out. I said you had to drive away over to Sandville to see Aunt Carrie who's sick and maybe you wouldn't even get back tonight." [For an incident in which a young man is trapped into proposing marriage.]

43 ADOPT AN APPROPRIATE MOOD, TONE, AND MANNER.

In writing, the manner may be as important as the matter. An appropriate manner recommends what the writer has to say; an inappropriate manner may nullify it. In any form of writing, the manner should be appropriate to the subject, to the occasion and the reader, and to the writer himself.

43 A Be simple and direct.

Express the thought in language as simple as possible. Do not use learned, multi-syllabic words if short, common words are as accurate and expressive. On the other hand, do not use several little words in lieu of a more expressive "big" word, unless you are writing for children, the uneducated, or the immature.

As a rule, approach the subject head-on. Do not write around it or come at it obliquely. Do not be coy. In other words, do not beat around the bush; come out with it.

Do not philosophize or pontificate about trivial matter. Only a pompous person or a fool will enlarge the magnitude of a thing and make a mountain out of a molehill.

43 B Strive to be accurate, clear, and emphatic.

Always ask three questions about every statement: Is it accurate? Is it clear? Is it emphatic? Accuracy, clarity, and emphasis are the essentials of effective writing.

Do not strive to display erudition or a large vocabulary. Do not strive to be original or poetic. Do not strive for style. Do not, in short, strive for "literary effect." Style does not come from posturing; it is the product of accuracy, clarity, and emphasis.

43 C   Be modest, unassuming, and temperate.

Do not pretend to know everything about a subject, large or small. Do not generalize from a limited knowledge of a subject. Having read only Sandburg among Lincoln's biographers, for example, do not say that Sandburg is the most reliable biographer of Lincoln. Say that Sandburg seems reliable. Above all, do not pretend to large knowledge in a subject you are just beginning to explore.

In a paper based on limited knowledge of a subject, do not be sarcastic, ironic, or otherwise scornful. Do not make accusations or judgments except within the limited area being scrutinized and then only with the greatest caution. Such arrogance and presumption are likely to be a boomerang.

Qualify statements and judgments. Say that things seem to be, or from your limited acquaintance appear to be. Say that in your opinion something is excellent; say that something is one of the best, or among the better, or it is the best that you know. There are numerous ways of qualifying a remark and avoiding the fatuous and irritating superlative.

43 D   Do not strive to be funny.

Many students of writing have the false notion that the reader always wants to be entertained and that comedy is the only form of entertainment. The writer who is always striving to be funny is as tiresome as the guest who is always striving to be the life of the party. In writing, as in life, humor is a spice, effective when used sparingly.

If it be true that everything has an element of comedy, the person who always finds it is a bore. Serious subjects should be treated seriously. In them an accompanying patter of jokes and humorous comments is disruptive and offensive. And furthermore, the humor is likely to be forced and foolish. The writer should let his purpose be his guide. If his purpose is to explain, to instruct, or to judge, humor is out of place. This is not to say that the treatment may not, at times, be light, but it does not have to be funny, and the writer should not strain to make it so.

If humorous touches are appropriate or if the purpose is to amuse, the paper may, of course, be funny. Beginners should take warning, however; humor is one of the hardest kinds of writing. It requires a special gift and consummate skill.

44 IN DESCRIPTIVE WRITING USE A PRINCIPLE OF ORGANIZATION.

Description is more than a catalogue of physical details. To make a definite picture and a definite impression, the details must be selected and arranged meaningfully.

44 A Use a fundamental image to help make description graphic.

A fundamental image is the basic form or outline of an object. For example, the design of a building is an "*H*" or a *cross;* Italy is shaped like a *boot.* The fundamental image offers several advantages. For the writer it provides a design on which he can establish the position of details and show how they are related to each other. For the reader, it compares the object to something familiar which he can immediately visualize, which he can hold in his mind, and to which he can refer the descriptive details.

The use of the fundamental image is illustrated by the following passage in which a street is likened in outline to a bent fish hook:

Ours is really a one-sided street that curves partly around the village green like a *bent fish hook.* On the *shank,* screened by a row of poplars, sits the Williams Manse, now abandoned and boarded up. At the middle of the *bend,* flanked by neat cottages, is the district school. Diagonally across the green, on the *barb of the hook* sits our house with a view of the green from the front porch and of the state highway from the rear.

44 B   **Use a fundamental impression to help make description unified and coherent.**

The first impression of anything is usually a fundamental impression. The observer perceives the object as a whole and makes an immediate judgment. Later he becomes aware of the details that contribute to the total effect.

A fundamental impression is the total effect of an object. A woman is *blowsy and vulgar*. A town is *rambling and squalid*. A room is *warm and cozy*. A day is *dreary*. Once the writer has stated the fundamental impression that an object makes, he can complete his description of it by presenting the details which create the impression. Thus the fundamental impression simplifies and clarifies the task of description. It is a principle according to which the writer can select pertinent details and around which he can arrange them. The fundamental impression is the purpose for writing the description.

In Herman Melville's *Typee* the fundamental impression of Mehevi is that of a superb-looking, imposing warrior. Note how this impression is stated and begins to take shape in the first paragraph of the description.

At last . . . a superb-looking warrior stooped the towering plumes of his head dress beneath the low portal and entered the house. I saw at once that he was some distinguished personage, the natives regarding him with the utmost deference, and making room for him as he approached. His aspect was imposing. The splendid long-drooping tail feathers of the tropical bird, thickly interspersed with the gaudy plumage of the cock, were disposed in an immense upright semi-circle upon his head, their lower extremities being fixed in a crescent of guinea beads which spanned the forehead. Around his neck were several enormous necklaces of boars tusks, polished like ivory, and disposed in such a manner that the longest and largest were upon his capacious chest. Thrust forward through the large apertures in his ears were two small and finely shaped sperm-whale teeth presenting their cavities in front, stuffed with freshly plucked leaves and curiously wrought at the other end into strange little images and devices. These barbaric trinkets, garnished in this manner at their open extremities, and tapering and curving round to a point behind the ear, resembled not a little a pair of cornucopias.

44 C Use a focal point as a means of organizing descriptive detail.

In description a focal point often helps the writer to arrange the details in a visual pattern. The focal point is usually the dominant feature of what is being described. The advantage of the focal point is that it establishes a center of interest, a fixed point which the reader as well as the writer can keep in mind and to which he can relate all of the other details. The focal point pulls the details together and arranges them in a design that is readily visualized.

The use of the focal point is illustrated in the following description of a summer camp. Here the focal point is the main house, and the rest of the camp is related to it.

When I was a boy, we spent our vacations at a fisherman's camp on Lake Obiscopee. The camp was situated on ten or twelve acres of pine land that curved like a broad ribbon around the lakefront. Above the lake in the center of the strip sat the main house. It was the dining room, the recreation room, and the office all in one, a haven where, on rainy days and cold nights, we played games in front of the large fireplace. From the porch overlooking the lake there was a piney view of the dock, the diving float, and the sandy beach where we children could swim unattended if there was a watcher above. Behind the main house stretched a large field, a good place to play ball or pick wild flowers and chase grasshoppers. The cabins were situated in the pines on either side of the main house, six on one side and five on the other, close to the lake and close to the dining room whither old Sam, the waiter, dishwasher, and general handyman, summoned us three times a day by rattling the cowbell on the porch.

45 PREPARING THE MANUSCRIPT

Neatness, legibility, and attractiveness of appearance should always be the writer's goals when preparing a paper to be submitted to an individual, a board or committee, a periodical, or a publisher. *Fair copy,* specified by most publishers, means a manuscript which is neat as well as correct. It is not required to be entirely free of erasures or corrections, but it is assumed that these will be held to a minimum and that there will be no difficulty in reading and no possibility of misreading.

Material of any sort submitted for publication should be accompanied by a letter. The letter need state only that you are submitting your work for consideration by the editor or publisher, or it may explain the nature of the work and point out any inducements for its publication, such as particular appeals for special groups of readers, the timeliness or importance of the topic, or any originality in your method of treatment.

45 A   PHYSICAL APPEARANCE

The manuscript should be written or typed on paper approximately 8½ x 11 inches, the standard size of typewriter paper and commercial letterheads. It should be typed, if possible, and double spaced throughout except for indented quotations which may be single spaced. (See 34 B.) If the manuscript is handwritten, lined paper should be used, the lines widely enough spaced to separate each line of writing clearly from the one above it and to avoid any suggestion of a cramped page. Whether the manuscript is typed or written, only one side of the paper should be used.

The first page should have the title at the top, followed by the author's name unless the mansucript is a report. Formal reports are concluded by the complimentary close *Respectfully submitted*, followed by the author's signature. Between the heading and the beginning of the text, extra space should be left, a line on ruled paper and at least a triple space on typewritten material.

THE CHANGING SEASONS
by
Arthur L. Kennedy

          The advent of each new spring serves to remind us that Mother Nature has gone out of her

way to see to it that we are not bored by any
monotony caused by her....

Indent the first and all succeeding paragraphs (five spaces is
customary for typescript), but do not leave extra space between paragraphs. After the opening page, all pages should be
numbered, preferably at the upper right hand corner of each
sheet. Page numbers may be placed at top center or bottom center
of each page, but the upper right hand corner position is preferable because it makes possible quick and easy reference to any
desired page.

45 B   USE AND POSITION OF FOOTNOTES

Footnotes are a requirement for a research paper and are occasionally needed for other kinds of writing. They are used to
acknowledge the borrowing of facts, statements, or quotations
from specific sources. They may also be used for adding to the
text explanations or supplementary material of any sort which
is not sufficiently important to be included in the text or which
would distract from the train of thought being developed in the
text. If very few footnotes are used, they may be indicated by
asterisks (*) or daggers (†), but it is usual and preferable
simply to use Arabic numerals placed slightly above the line at
the end of the quotations or statements for which references are
given.[1] In a book of several chapters or other divisions, the
footnotes may be numbered consecutively throughout the text,
or a new numerical sequence may be introduced for each chapter or section after the first. If there are a great many footnotes,
the latter method is preferable simply to keep the footnote
numerals from reaching into the hundreds and consuming unnecessary space. As the name implies, the footnotes themselves
are usually placed at the foot or the bottom of the page on
which the indications are made. They should be clearly de-

[1] This is an example of an explanatory footnote. The footnote numeral
always follows any punctuation occurring at the point of its insertion. The
first word of any footnote is capitalized.

marked from the text itself either by a solid line or by additional space separating them from the text. If the manuscript is to be submitted for publication, all of the footnotes should be placed together and appended to the text as a separate section. The printer will place them on the pages where they belong. (Footnotes are occasionally placed at the end of the article or book or at the end of each chapter or other division. This position makes the writing, typing, or printing easier, but it inconveniences the reader.)

45 C   FORM OF FOOTNOTES— PRIMARY REFERENCE

When the first reference to a source is given, complete information about it should be included in the footnote (unless a bibliography is to be appended at the end of the work): the author, the title, the volume and edition (if there is more than one edition), and the page number. The place and date of publication and the name of the publisher should also be given.

1. John Macalister, *The Golden Gate*, 4th ed. (New York: John Horton & Co., 1914), III, 312.

This footnote indicates page 312 of Volume III of the fourth edition of a book entitled *The Golden Gate* written by John Macalister and published in New York by John Horton & Co. in 1914. If the volume does not contain a date of publication, the date of copyright is used. If no date at all can be found, the abbreviation *n.d.* (no date) is used. If no place of publication is given, the abbreviation *n.p.* means *no place*. Assuming these unusual circumstances for the above mentioned work, the footnote would read:

1. John Macalister, *The Golden Gate*, 4th ed. (n.p., n.d.), III, 312.

If a bibliography is to be added at the end of the work, only the minimum of information required to identify each reference need be given. The previous footnote would then read:

1. John Macalister, *The Golden Gate,* 4th ed., III, 312.

If the reference is not to a particular volume of a work, it is customary to insert the abbreviation *p.* for *page* or *pp.* for *pages.*

1. James Nelson, *Automation in the Textile Industry* (Chicago: Dunn & Co., 1959), p. 57. [or pp. 57-61.]

If there are two or more authors, their names should be listed as they occur on the title page of the book.

1. John French and Samuel D. Barton, *The New Dispensation* (Dublin: Standish & Sons, 1929), pp. 32-46.

If the source involves an editor or translator, this information should be given as follows:

1. William Shakespeare, *Hamlet,* ed. John Hurd (Boston: Alan Sims, 1870), p. 27.

2. Giovanni Boccaccio, *The Decameron,* trans. Ann Minter (New York: Dawson & Co., 1860), p. 47.

If the source is a collection of some sort which involves an editor only instead of an author, this information is conveyed as follows:

1. Thomas Diston (ed.), *Life Insurance Tables for Actuaries* (Cambridge, Mass.: The College Press, 1950), p. 68.

If the reference is to a source which occurs within a magazine, a newspaper, or as part of a larger work, the following usages are employed:

A signed newspaper article:

1. John Smart, "The Rising Tax Rate," The New York *Times* (February 8, 1912), p. 12.

An unsigned newspaper article (and indication of the section of the paper):

1. "The Rising Tax Rate," The Memphis *Star* (March 4, 1952), Sec. 2, p. 3.

A newspaper editorial:

> 1. "The Rising Tax Rate" (editorial), The London *Gazette* (April 7, 1936), p. 14.

A section of a book:

> 1. Jennifer West, "Search for a Father," *Thirty Famous Short Stories,* ed. Frederick Noble (New York: Eaton & Co., 1916), pp. 72-93.

An encyclopedia article:

> 1. "Textiles," *Encyclopaedia Brittanica*, 9th ed., XXIII, 206-7.

(If the article is signed, the author's name should also be given.)

A story or an article in a magazine:

> 1. John Crow, "The Wayward Child," *The Atlantic Monthly* (June, 1944), pp. 8-11.

If the magazine has numbered issues, this information may be included, but the date should always be given if available:

> 1. Jennifer Finch, "The Golden Harvest," *The Farmer's Quarterly*, III, 3 (Autumn, 1940), pp. 36-48.

If the reference is to a speech or some kind of performance, all pertinent information should be given.

> 1. John Norton, "The Wavering Trust," sermon preached at the West End Tabernacle, Dayton, Ohio, Sept. 3, 1943.

45 D   FORM OF FOOTNOTES— SECONDARY REFERENCE

When exact reference has been made to a source, subsequent references (unless appearing after a considerable interval) may give the minimum of information required to identify the source. If a second reference is made to the same source and page immediately after the original citation, the abbreviation *ibid.* (*ibidem*—"in the same place") is all that is necessary. If the reference is to another part of the same work, the new page number, or the new page and volume number, should be added. Repetition of the identical reference:

1. Mary Watkins, *The Culture of the Aztecs* (Paris: The Little Press, 1914), IV, 27.

2. Ibid.

Reference to another part of the same work:

1. Mary Watkins, *The Culture of the Aztecs* (Paris: The Little Press, 1914), IV, 27.

2. Ibid., II, 423.

Ibid. refers always to the note *immediately above.* If the second reference to a source occurs after one or more intervening references to other sources have been made, the reference may be abbreviated to include only the author's surname and the page number.

1. Howard Lansing, *The Lost Cause* (New Orleans: James Sutton & Co., 1950), III, 27.

2. James Harlow, *The Opening Wedge* (Chicago: Little Books, 1912), p. 43.

3. Lansing, II, 134.

45 E ABBREVIATIONS

As a general rule, abbreviations of any kind should be avoided in the text of an article, but they are customary in footnotes and bibliographies. It was formerly standard procedure to put abbreviations of Latin or other foreign words in italics, but these abbreviations are so well known that they may be said to have become completely anglicized. Consequently, the practice of placing them in italics has almost completely died out and will not be followed here.

The following are the most common abbreviations:

anon. anonymous—used in place of author of an anonymous work

art., arts. "article, articles"

b. "born"—used to indicate date of birth.

bibliog. "bibliography"

biog. "biography"

bk., bks. "book, books"

ca. (or c.) *circa*—"*about*." c. *1909* means *about 1909*

cf. "confer"—meaning compare

ch., chs. "chapter, chapters"

col., cols. "column, columns"—for reference to the columns of print on a page

d. "died"

diss. "dissertation"

ed., eds., "editor, editors"—or "edition, editions"—or "edited by"

e. g. *exempli gratia*—for example (preceded and followed by commas)

esp. "especially"

et al. *et. alia*—"and others"—as in a volume with many authors: *Smith, Houston, Jones, et al.*

et seq. *et sequens*—"and the following"

etc. *et cetera*—"and so forth"

f., ff. and the following line or page, lines or pages

fig., figs. "figure, figures"—usually referring to illustrations

fl. *floruit*—"flourished," followed by a date to denote the high point of an individual's achievement, principally used when dates of birth and death are uncertain

ibid., ib., id., idem *ibidem*—"in the same place"

i. e. *id est*—"that is"—preceded and followed by commas

infra "below"—used to refer to following material

introd. "introduction" or "introduction by"

l., ll. "line, lines"—used to refer to lines of poetry or similar text where exact reference is required

loc. cit. *loco citato*—"in the place cited"—in the place cited in a recent note

MS, MSS, MS., MSS., ms, mss, ms., mss. (capitalized or not, with or without period) "manuscript, manuscripts"

N. B. or n. b. *nota bene*—"note well"—to alert attention to what follows

n. d. "no date"—to explain failure to supply date of publication

no., nos. "number, numbers"

n. p. "no place" of publication given

op. cit. *opere citato*—"in the work cited"

p., pp. "page, pages"

par., pars. "paragraph, paragraphs"

passim "here and there"—used to indicate material that occurs here and there throughout a work

pseud. "pseudonym"

pub. "published" or "publication"

pubs. "publications"

sic "so"—usually placed in brackets to indicate that a seeming mistake is copied from the original work: "*It was thiers* [*sic*]."

trans. or tr. "translator" or "translation" or "translated by"

viz. *videlicet*—"it is permitted to see"—namely—preceded and followed by commas

vol., vols. "volume, volumes"

vs. *versus*—"against"

45 F   BIBLIOGRAPHY

Placed at the end of the work, the bibliography is usually the list of sources referred to in the body of the text or in the footnotes, or both. Sometimes, it may consist of works connected with the subject, whether referred to in the text or not. In either case, the listing is in alphabetical order and follows the plan for each entry of author, title, place of publication, name of publisher, and date of publication. If there is no author, the title of the piece is listed in its correct alphabetical position in the bibliography. If two or more works by the same author are listed, the author's name is not repeated, but succeeding titles by the same author are indented. For very well known works like the *Encyclopaedia Brittannica*, information about place and date of publication is usually omitted.

SAMPLE BIBLIOGRAPHY

Anderson, W. J. and Spiers, R. P., The Architecture of Greece and Rome, 2 vols. New York: Scribner, 1927.

Antcliffe, Herbert, "Music in the Life of the Ancient Greeks." Musical Quarterly, April, 1930, pp. 40–54.

Baker, Russell, "Kennedy Decries Big Soviet Gains." The New York Times, November 14, 1959, p. 10, col. 6.

Lee, Edwin A., "Vocational Education." Encyclopedia Americana, 1950, XXVIII, 160–161.

"Making Your Own Clothes." The Young Lady's Magazine, April, 1870, pp. 19–28.

Muir, Ramsey, The Expansion of Europe. Boston: Houghton Mifflin, 1928.

—Nationalism and Internationalism. Boston: Houghton Mifflin, 1917.

Newton, A. P., ed., Travel and Travellers in the
    Middle Ages. New York: Knopf, 1926.

Rousseau, Jean Jacques, The Social Contract and
    Discourses, trans. G. D. H. Cole. London
    and New York: E. P. Dutton & Co.   (Everyman's
    Library), 1913.

45 G   A SAMPLE RESEARCH PAPER

Although the material in this paper is drawn from an actual
book, many of the references are deliberately artificial to illustrate different types of footnotes. The first two footnotes will
assume that no bibliography follows the article. The remaining
footnotes will give only the information required of footnotes
when a bibliography is to be appended.

PRIMITIVE NUMBER SYMBOLISM
by
John L. Doe

Nothing in the history of number symbolism is
so striking as the unanimity of all ages and
climates in regard to the meanings of a certain
few number symbols. Inasmuch as these same
number beliefs color the literature of the
ancient world and recur in the superstitions of
contemporary primitive peoples, we are justified
in classifying them as elementary or primitive
symbols.[1]

An examination of these earliest number symbols indicates that numbers originally carried
concrete associations, as a result of man's
early inability to comprehend abstractions.
Such a hypothesis is in keeping with the recog-
nizable trend of language from the concrete to

1.   Cf. John D. Elder, Primitivism, Yesterday
    and Today (New York: Hamlin & Co., 1943),
    passim.

the abstract,[2] and is demonstrable in the commonplace method of teaching addition and subtraction by the aid of concrete illustration.
These associations must originally have been
more real than the number itself, three trees
more real than the abstract number three, so
that particularly prominent and fixed numerical
groups might readily come to be thought of as
the attributes of the numbers themselves. In
ancient Babylon, as Cumont points out,

> a number was a very different thing from a
> figure. Just as in ancient times, and above
> all, in Egypt the name had a magic power,...
> so here the number possesses an active force,
> the number is a symbol, and its properties
> are sacred attributes.[3]

Presumably every early civilization once
passed through a stage today duplicated in certain Brazilian tribes whose languages are almost
completely barren of number words.[4] One tribe
uses only the word etama, alone, to indicate a
single object or one of a group. The first advance toward counting develops the use of words
for one and many, the differentiation of the
individual from the group.[5]

But man must soon have become conscious of the
duals of nature: male and female, day and night,

2. Joyce Lermont, "Some Observations on Primitive Languages," The Linguistic Review
    (April, 1930), pp. 42-58.
3. Franz Cumont, Astrology and Religion among
    the Greeks and Romans, pp. 29-30.
4. Levi Leonard Conant, The Number Concept,
    p. 1.
5. Ibid., pp. 1, 22, 24, 28; Edward B. Tylor,
    Primitive Culture, I, 243.

sun and moon. Doubtless Alcmaeon of Crotona was repeating a very common observation when he remarked that "most human things go in pairs."[6] It is probable, then, that the early mathematician chose some noteworthy duality of nature, such as marriage, as his word for two. At any rate, the number two appears always to have carried with it the idea of mutual antithesis found in the duals of nature, whether in the great Manichean duad or in the double head of the Egyptian Horus "whereof the one beareth right and truth and the other wickedness."[7]

Having invented a term for "pair," man was in possession of three numerical terms, one, two, many, and there are tribes today who count in just such a fashion.[8] Through some process not clearly traceable, there came to be an identification of the word for many with the concept of three. This stage is reflected in the distinction between the dual and the plural in the Egyptian, Arabian, Hebrew, Sanskrit, Greek, and Gothic languages,[9] and in the common use of positive, comparative, and superlative degrees.

The idea of three as implying the superlative, or the all, was never lost. It appears in such common phrases as ter felix ("thrice happy"), in the use of the trident and triple thunderbolt as symbols of greatness and power, in the Egyptian hieroglyphs, where a single bar marking the picture of an object indicates but one, a double bar two, but three lines indicate three or an indefinite number of objects.[10]

6. Aristotle, Metaphysics, I, 5.
7. Book of the Dead, XCII, 28.
8. Conant, p. 22; D. E. Smith, History of Mathematics, I, 6, 9; Tylor, I, 243.
9. Tylor, I, 265.
10. Ibid.

The persistence of this half—instinctive mode of reasoning is one of the curiosities of human logic. Erastosthenes (c. 240 B.C.) observes that "the gods vouchsafe moral improvement to those who have thrice wiped themselves clean."[11] Legends, myths, folk tales of all nations abound in three wishes, three tries, three suitors— there is no necessity for prolonging the story when three is all. In the Old Testament we are told that "a threefold cord is not quickly broken."[12] The medieval theologian makes a point of the three days entombment of Christ, "for in three days is proved all deed and fait veritable."[13] Lewis Carroll was possibly hinting at the frailty of even modern scientific minds in accepting three examples as proof when he has the Bellman gravely announce, "What I tell you three times is true."

The triplicity of rising, midday, and setting sun provides another instance where three is all: beginning, middle, end. In the human cycle, to go no further in search of analogies, birth, life, and death represent the triple division which is common to all mundane affairs, recognized in the Greek Fates and the Scandinavian Norns. In Indian theology, Brahma, Vishnu, and Siva are similarly disposed. In a fragment of the Orphic theogony, Zeus is described as the beginning, middle, and end of all things.[14]

11. Frederick Cornwallis Conybeare, Myth, Magic and Morals, p. 318.
12. Ecclesiastes 4:12.
13. Legenda aurea, Resurrection (Temple Classics), pp. 87–88.
14. Eduard Zeller, A History of Greek Philosophy, I, 64.

From early associations of this kind with specific numbers, there were gradually developed many different types of elaborate and complex number symbolisms, some of which died with medieval magic and various mystical cults but many of which survive to the present day.

GLOSSARY OF WORDS AND
PHRASES FREQUENTLY MISUSED

G 1 a, an Use *a* before words beginning with a consonant sound: *a book, a unique necklace.* Use *an* before words beginning with a vowel sound: *an apple, an urchin.* (See 4 B.)

G 2 accept, except *Accept* means to receive: "Please *accept* my offer." The verb *except* means to leave out: "Will you *except* the last provision of the contract?"

G 3 adverse, averse *Adverse* means *opposing: adverse circumstances. Averse* means *disinclined:* "He was *averse* to my proposal." *Adverse* is usually related to actions or things, *averse* to people (who have an aversion).

G 4 advert, avert *Advert* means *refer:* "The speaker *adverted* to an earlier talk he had given." *Avert* means *ward off:* "He narrowly *averted* a bad fall."

G 5 affect, effect *Affect* means *to influence:* "His attitude in class *affected* his grade." *Affect* is never used as a noun except in psychological terminology. *Effect* as a noun means *result:* "The *effect* of the explosion was disastrous." *Effect* as a verb means *to accomplish:* "The new machinery *effected* a decided improvement in the product."

G 6 aggravate Do not use *aggravate* to mean *irritate. Aggravate* means to make a bad situation worse.

G 7 alright Illiterate for *all right.* Do not confuse the spelling with words like *almost, already, altogether.*

G 8 alumnus, alumna, alumni, alumnae An *Alumnus* is a male graduate. *Alumni* is the plural. An *alumna* is a female graduate. *Alumnae* is the plural. *Alumni* is used for male and female combined.

G 9 among, between *Between* is used in connection with two persons or things: "He divided the money *between* his two sons." *Among* is used for more than two: "He divided the money *among* his three sons." EXCEPTIONS: If more than two are involved in a united situation, *between* is used: "*Between* the four of us we raised a thousand dollars." If a comparison or an opposition is involved, *between* is used: "There was great rivalry *between* the three colleges. It was difficult to choose *between* them."

G 10 amount, number *Amount* refers to bulk or quantity: *amount* of sugar, grain, flour, money. *Number* refers to objects which are thought of as individual units: *number* of oranges, children, diamonds. Notice that most words following *amount* are singular (*coal, butter, water*) and that most words following *number* are plural (*apples, bottles, cups*).

G 11 apt, liable, likely *Apt* refers to a habitual disposition: "Having a good brain, he is *apt* to get high grades." *Likely* merely expresses probability: "It is *likely* to rain." *Liable* implies the probability of something unfortunate: "The firm is *liable* to fail."

G 12 as, like When used as a preposition, *like* should never introduce a clause (NOT *like I was saying*). When introducing a clause, *as* is used (*as I was saying*) even if some of the words of the clause are implied: "He did it as well *as* I [did]." (See 7 D.)

G 13 beside, besides *Beside* means *by the side of:* "Ask him to sit *beside* me." *Besides* means *in addition:* "She was an expert secretary. *Besides,* she had a wonderful disposition."

G 14 bring, take *Bring* refers to action toward the writer or speaker: "*Bring* the book to me." *Take* refers to action away from the writer or speaker: "When you leave us, *take* your books with you."

G 15 can, may *Can* implies ability: "I *can* (am able to) swim." *May* denotes permission: "*May* I (Have I permission to) swim in your pool?"

G 16 claim, assert *Claim* refers to a justified demand or legal right: "I *claim* this piece of property." "I *claim* the prize." It should not be used when only an assertion is involved: "He *asserted* (not *claimed*) that his demands were reasonable."

G 17 compare to, compare with *Compare to* is used to indicate a definite resemblance: "He compared the railroad *to* a street." *Compare with* is used to indicate an examination of similarities and dissimilarities: "He compared the middle ages *with* modern times."

G 18 counsel, council *Counsel* as a noun means *advice,* or, in legal parlance, a lawyer or lawyers: "He sought my *counsel.*" "He retained *counsel* to represent him at the trial."

As a verb *counsel* means *to advise:* "I would *counsel* you to accept the first good offer." *Council* is a *group* of individuals who act in an advisory capacity or who meet for the purposes of discussion or decision-making: "The mayor met with the *council*." "They called a *council* to make plans for the future."

G 19 different from *Different from* is the correct idiom, NOT *different than.*

G 20 differ from, differ with *Differ from* applies to differences between one person or thing and others: "My car *differs from* his because it is a newer model." *Differ with* means to have a difference in opinion: "I *differ with* him in his views about government."

G 21 don't *Don't* is the contraction of *do not: I don't, you don't, we don't, they don't.* Do not confuse it with *doesn't,* the contraction of *does not: He doesn't, she doesn't, it doesn't.*

G 22 due to *Due to* acts grammatically as an adjective and must therefore modify a specific noun or pronoun: "The *flood* was *due to* the rapid spring thaw." If there is no specific noun for *due* to modify, use the phrase *because of:* "He was late *because of* an accident." Or rephrase the sentence: "His *lateness* was *due to* an accident."

G 23 fewer, less *Fewer* is used in connection with people or with objects which are thought of as individual units: *fewer oranges, fewer children, fewer books, fewer dollars. Less* is used in connection with the concept of bulk: *less money, less coal, less weight, less grain.* Notice that most words following *fewer* are plural (*oranges, books, dollars*); most words following *less* are singular (*money, coal, wheat*).

G 24 former, latter *Former* and *latter* are used to designate one of *two* persons or things: "Of the *two* possibilities, I prefer the *former* to the *latter*." If more than two persons or things are involved, *first* or *first named* and *last* or *last named* are used: "He had a choice of yellow, rose, pink, and brown. He preferred the *first* and *last* to the others."

G 25 had ought *Ought* is known as a defective verb because it has only one form and cannot be used with an auxiliary: "They *ought* (NOT *had ought*) to have told her."

G 26 hanged, hung *Hanged* is used in connection with executions: "He was condemned to be *hanged* by the neck until dead." *Hung* denotes any other kind of suspension: "The pictures were *hung* on the wall."

G 27 hardly Like *barely* and *scarcely*, *hardly* should not be used with a negative. "He was *hardly* (*barely*, *scarcely*) able to do it." (NOT *not hardly*, *barely*, *scarcely*)

G 28 healthful, healthy *Healthful* means *health-giving: a healthful climate*. *Healthy* means *in a state of health:* "He was a *healthy* young man."

G 29 imply, infer *Imply* means to throw out a hint or suggestion: "She *implied* by her manner that she was unhappy." *Infer* means to take in a hint or suggestion: "I *inferred* from her manner that she was unhappy."

G 30 its, it's *Its* (no apostrophe) is the possessive case of *it:* "The pig nursed *its* young." *It's* is the contraction for *it is:* "*It's* too late to do anything about it." (See 2A.)

G 31 kind, sort, type, variety Since these words are singular in number, they should never be prefaced by plural modifiers: *This kind of people* (NOT *these kind of people*).

G 32 kind of, sort of, type of, variety of Never place an article after these expressions: *this kind of pistol* (NOT *this kind of a pistol*). (See 1 B.)

G 33 lay, lie *Lay, laid, laid* are the principal parts of the transitive verb which means *to put down:* "I shall *lay* the rug." "I *laid* the rug." "I *have laid* the rug." *Lie, lay, lain* are the principal parts of the intransitive verb (it cannot take an object) which means *to recline* or *repose:* "She *will lie* in the hammock." "She *is lying* in the hammock." "She *lay* in the hammock yesterday." "She *has lain* there all afternoon."

G 34 lead, led When pronounced alike, the noun *lead* is the metal, *led* is the past tense and past participle of the verb *to lead*.

G 35 learn, teach *Learn* means to acquire information or knowledge: "I *learned* my lesson." *Teach* means to impart information or knowledge: "I *taught* him to do it."

G 36 liable See *apt* (G 11).

G 37 like See *as* (G 12).

G 38 militate, mitigate *Militate* (connected with *military*) means to have strong influence for or against, usually against: "His grouchy manner *militated* against his success as a salesman." *Mitigate* means to *lessen:* "The cold compress on his leg *mitigated* his suffering."

G 39 **myself** *Myself* (like *yourself, himself, herself, itself, themselves*) is an intensive and reflexive pronoun. It should never be used in a sentence without its corresponding noun or pronoun: "*I myself* will do it." "*I* hurt *myself*." "They sent for John and *me* (NOT *myself*). (See 2 F.)

G 40 **principal, principle** *Principal* is usually an adjective: *principal cities, principal people*. It has become a noun in a few usages where the noun it formerly modified has been dropped. "He was the *principal* (teacher) of the school." "I withdrew the *principal* (amount) and interest from my savings account." "He acted as the *principal* (person) rather than as an agent." In every other usage, the noun *principle* means a basic law or doctrine: "The country was founded on the *principle* that all men are created equal."

G 41 **reason is because** The words *reason is* (*was,* etc.) should be followed by a statement of the reason: "The reason for his failure was illness." "The reason for the strict rules is to enforce discipline." Similar statements can be made by using *because:* "He failed because of illness." "The rules are strict because it is necessary to enforce discipline." *Reason* and *because* convey the same sense. It is illogical to use both words to convey the same meaning.

G 42 **same** Do not use *same* as a pronoun: "I have your order for the books and will send them (NOT will send same)."

G 43 **their, there** Be careful to distinguish the spelling of the possessive case of the pronoun *their* (*their books*) from the spelling of the adverb and expletive *there*. "I got *there* before I knew it." "*There* are forty grapefruit in the crate."

G 44 **therefor, therefore** *Therefor* means *for that, for it, for them:* "I sent the manuscript by registered mail and have the receipt *therefor*." *Therefore* means *for that reason:* "He was sick. *Therefore* he did not go to work."

G 45 **unique** *Unique* means the only one of its kind: "His was a *unique* personality." It cannot logically be used in a comparative or superlative form. Something may be more or most odd, rare, unusual, peculiar, remarkable, etc., but NOT more or most unique.

G 46 who's, whose *Who's* is the contraction for *who is* and *who has:* "I cannot imagine *who's* coming." *Whose* is the possessive form of *who:* "We knew the family *whose* house was robbed." (See 2 B.)

G 47 woman, women Just as the plural of *man* is *men,* so the plural of *woman* is *women.*

·CONJUGATIONS AND PRINCIPAL PARTS

Conjugation of the Verb *To Be*

Infinitive: to be, be
Perfect Infinitive: to have been
Present Participle: being
Present Perfect Participle: having been
Past Participle: been

INDICATIVE MOOD

Person	Singular	Plural

Present Tense

Person	Singular	Plural
First	I am	we are
Second	you are	you are
Third	he (she, it) is	they are

Future Tense

First	I shall be	we shall be
Second	you will be	you will be
Third	he (she, it) will be	they will be

Past Tense

First	I was	we were
Second	you were	you were
Third	he (she, it) was	they were

CONJUGATIONS AND PRINCIPAL PARTS

Present Perfect Tense

First	I have been	we have been
Second	you have been	you have been
Third	he (she, it) has been	they have been

Past Perfect Tense

First	I had been	we had been
Second	you had been	you had been
Third	he (she, it) had been	they had been

Future Perfect Tense

First	I shall have been	we shall have been
Second	you will have been	you will have been
Third	he (she, it) will have been	they will have been

IMPERATIVE MOOD

be

SUBJUNCTIVE MOOD

Present Tense: if I (you, he, she, it, we, they) be
Past Tense: if I (you, he, she, it, we, they) were

Conjugation of the Verb *To Drive*

ACTIVE VOICE	PASSIVE VOICE
Infinitive: to drive, drive	to be driven, be driven
Perfect Infinitive: to have driven	to have been driven
Present Particple: driving	being driven
Perfect Participle: having driven	having been driven
Past Participle: driven	been driven

CONJUGATIONS AND PRINCIPAL PARTS

INDICATIVE MOOD

Present Tense

Singular	Plural	Singular	Plural
1. I drive	we drive	I am driven	we are driven
2. you drive	you drive	you are driven	you are driven
3. he (she, it) drives	they drive	he (she, it) is driven	they are driven

Future Tense

1. I shall drive	we shall drive	I shall be driven	we shall be driven
2. you will drive	you will drive	you will be driven	you will be driven
3. he will drive	they will drive	he will be driven	they will be driven

Past Tense

1. I drove	we drove	I was driven	we were driven
2. you drove	you drove	you were driven	you were driven
3. he drove	they drove	he was driven	they were driven

Present Perfect Tense

1. I have driven	we have driven	I have been driven	we have been driven
2. you have driven	you have driven	you have been driven	you have been driven
3. he has driven	they have driven	he has been driven	they have been driven

Past Perfect Tense

1. I had driven	we had driven	I had been driven	we had been driven
2. you had driven	you had driven	you had been driven	you had been driven
3. he had driven	they had driven	he had been driven	they had been driven

Future Perfect Tense

1. I shall have driven	we shall have driven	I shall have been driven	we shall have been driven
2. you will have driven	you will have driven	you will have been driven	you will have been driven
3. he will have driven	they will have driven	he will have been driven	they will have been driven

IMPERATIVE MOOD

drive

SUBJUNCTIVE MOOD

Present Tense

if I (you, he, she, it, we, they) drive   if I (you, he, she, it, we, they) be driven

Past Tense

if I (you, he, she, it, we, they) drove   if I (you, he, she, it, we, they) were driven

Principal Parts of Irregular Verbs

Regular verbs form the past tense and past participle by adding *ed* (*discover—discovered, cry—cried*) or *d* (*raise—raised, lay— laid*) to the infinitive. Verbs which do not follow these principles are known as irregular verbs. The following is a list of the principal parts of the most frequently used irregular verbs.

Infinitive and Present Tense	Past Tense	Past Participle
arise	arose	arisen
awake	awoke, awaked	awaked, awoke
bear	bore	borne (born—passive voice)
beat	beat	beaten
begin	began	begun
bend	bent	bent
bid (offer)	bid	bid
bid (command)	bade	bidden
bind	bound	bound
bite	bit	bitten, bit
blow	blew	blown
break	broke	broken
bring	brought	brought
broadcast	broadcast, broadcasted	broadcast, broadcasted
build	built	built
burst	burst	burst
buy	bought	bought
cast	cast	cast
catch	caught	caught
choose	chose	chosen
cling	clung	clung
come	came	come
creep	crept	crept
deal	dealt	dealt
dive	dived, dove	dived
do	did	done
draw	drew	drawn
drink	drank	drunk
drive	drove	driven
eat	ate	eaten
fall	fell	fallen
feed	fed	fed

CONJUGATIONS AND PRINCIPAL PARTS

Infinitive and Present Tense	Past Tense	Past Participle
feel	felt	felt
fight	fought	fought
find	found	found
flee	fled	fled
fling	flung	flung
fly	flew	flown
forbear	forbore	forborne
forbid	forbade, forbad	forbidden
forget	forgot	forgotten, forgot
forgive	forgave	forgiven
forsake	forsook	forsaken
freeze	froze	frozen
get	got	got, gotten
give	gave	given
go	went	gone
grow	grew	grown
hang	hung (hanged—executed)	hung (hanged—executed)
have (has)	had	had
hit	hit	hit
hold	held	held
hurt	hurt	hurt
kneel	knelt, kneeled	knelt
know	knew	known
lead	led	led
leap	leaped, leapt,	leaped, leapt
leave	left	left
lend	lent	lent
let	let	let
lie	lay	lain
lose	lost	lost
make	made	made

Infinitive and Present Tense	Past Tense	Past Participle
meet	met	met
put	put	put
read	read	read
rend	rent	rent
ride	rode	ridden
ring	rang	rung
rise	rose	risen
run	ran	run
see	saw	seen
seek	sought	sought
sell	sold	sold
send	sent	sent
set	set	set
shine	shone	shone
shrink	shrank, shrunk	shrunk, shrunken
sing	sang	sung
sink	sank	sunk
slay	slew	slain
sit	sat	sat
sleep	slept	slept
slide	slid	slid
sling	slung	slung
slink	slunk	slunk
speak	spoke	spoken
spring	sprang, sprung	sprung
steal	stole	stolen
stick	stuck	stuck
sting	stung	stung
stride	strode	strode, stridden
strike	struck	struck
swear	swore	sworn
sweat	sweat, sweated	sweated

CONJUGATIONS AND PRINCIPAL PARTS

Infinitive and Present Tense	Past Tense	Past Participle
sweep	swept	swept
swim	swam	swum
swing	swung	swung
take	took	taken
teach	taught	taught
tear	tore	torn
tell	told	told
think	thought	thought
thrive	throve, thrived	thrived, thriven
throw	threw	thrown
wake	waked, woke	waked, woken
wear	wore	worn
weep	wept	wept
win	won	won
wind	wound	wound
work	worked, wrought	worked, wrought
wring	wrung	wrung
write	wrote	written

·INDEX